The message in this book is so potent that it could incite a revolution of thought, heart, and action in the Body of Christ! We've experienced a Reformation in the Church, but now it's time for a Kingly Invasion to come forth. Kris Vallotton's goal is to demolish the "slave mind-set" and thrust true believers forward into authentic faith, power, and impact. *The Supernatural Ways of Royalty* will change your life!

—James W. Goll
Co-founder of Encounters Network
Author of *The Seer, The Lost Art of Intercession,*
and *The Coming Prophetic Revolution*

Kris Vallotton is one of the most remarkable people I have ever known. I expected his book to be remarkable and indeed it is. It is impossible to detect the borders of his life, message, and mission. In Kris all three comprise one stunning and beautiful adventure. The reader is assured here of a life-changing experience. Enjoy!

—Jack Taylor
President of Dimensions Ministries Melbourne, Florida

The Supernatural Ways of Royalty is destined to become a classic and is very timely in a world where there is little to hope for. This book is filled with hope that transports one from the darkness of distress to destiny…it is a must-read.

—Dr. Myles Munroe
CEO, Bahamas Faith Ministry
Author of *Rediscovering the Kingdom*

Kris Vallotton is a pastor with an unusually powerful prophetic gifting. He is also a friend—a friend of God, a friend to Heidi and me, and an intimate, intensely valued friend to ministry school students and hungry seekers of God everywhere who have experienced the joy of being touched by God through Kris's heart.

Readers of this book will be moved in the depths of their beings by Kris's revelation of the love of God as they have never understood it.

He unveils the true Gospel that elevates the redeemed to sonship and royalty, in the process bringing hearts to life that have been weighted down by rejection and oppression.

—Rolland and Heidi Baker
Iris Ministries

Wow! The enemy is really going to hate this book! That makes me love *The Supernatural Ways of Royalty* all the more! Once again, master storyteller, Kris Vallotton, along with Bill Johnson, are truly successful at showing you scripturally that from the moment you receive Christ, you've not just bought some land, but instead, God simply handed you the deed to the whole farm—and you didn't even ask Him for it. You own it all! Without your knowing it, you are the king, the CEO, the boss, in your Kingdom inheritance with all the benefits that satan hopes you don't discover. This book will teach you to live the abundant life that God has pre-ordained for you, if you will only embrace it.

—Steve Shultz
The Elijah List www.elijahlist.com

THE SUPERNATURAL
WAYS OF ROYALTY

THE SUPERNATURAL
WAYS OF ROYALTY

by

KRIS VALLOTTON

and

BILL JOHNSON

Destiny Image® **Publishers, Inc.**
P.O. Box 310
Shippensburg, PA 17257-0310

"Speaking to the Purposes of God for this Generation
and for the Generations to Come."

For Worldwide Distribution, Printed in the U.S.A.

ISBN 10: 0-7684-2323-6

ISBN 13: 978-0-7684-2323-5

13 14 15 / 16 15 14 13

This book and all other Destiny Image, Revival Press, MercyPlace, Fresh Bread, Destiny Image Fiction, and Treasure House books are available at Christian bookstores and distributors worldwide.

For a U.S. bookstore nearest you, call
1-800-722-6774.

For more information on foreign distributors, call
717-532-3040.

Or reach us on the Internet:
www.destinyimage.com

DEDICATION

I dedicate this book
to all the Saints of the world
who, like Joseph,
are trying to find their way
out of prison
and into the palace.

Then Samuel explained to the people the behavior of royalty, and wrote it in a book and laid it up before the Lord

(1 Samuel 10:25).

TABLE OF CONTENTS

FOREWORD

THROUGHOUT history great moves of God have rocked entire nations of the world. Each outpouring of the Spirit added necessary insights and experiences that have helped in restoring the Church to her eternal purpose. But coinciding with the new passion and mass conversions God always added another factor: another element of offense. It seems to be God's way. It is His way of separating the casual from the passionate, the hungry from the satisfied. For the desperate, "every bitter thing is sweet." God is building His people into His likeness through the fires of revival.

The outpouring of the Spirit always brings an increased awareness of our sinfulness. Some of the greatest hymns of confession and contrition have been written during such seasons. But the revelation of our sin and unworthiness is only half of the needed equation. Most revivals don't get past this one point, and therefore cannot sustain a move of God until it becomes a lifestyle. It's difficult to build something substantial on a negative. The other half of the equation is how holy He is on our behalf. When this is realized, our identity changes and our faith embraces the purpose of our salvation. At some point we must go beyond being simply "sinners saved by grace." As we learn to live out of our position in Christ we will bring forth the greatest exploits of all time. What one generation could accomplish from this one revelation is far beyond comprehension.

The Supernatural Ways of Royalty is an answer to such a heart cry—a cry lifted up by the church, by God Himself, and even by nature (see Rom. 8). Kris Vallotton takes us on a fearfully exciting journey through his testimony and the fresh revelations from Scripture that made it possible. Few have traveled this way before. Some reject it for fear of becoming proud and have chosen perpetual immaturity as a result. Much of what we desire in life is found in the tension of conflicting realities. Therefore, to the weak in faith, confidence appears to be arrogance. Faith must rise beyond the recognized norm into a lifestyle that accurately represents the victorious Son of God. We must trust God's ability to keep us more than we trust the devil's ability to deceive.

Kris and I have walked together in covenant for nearly 28 years. I have watched this revelation transform a man and have seen God's healing grace poured out on a broken life. Today Kris serves the Body of Christ as an unusually gifted man, a living testimony of God's strength being "perfected in weakness."

This book is necessary reading for all who desire to go beyond the status quo, beyond the comfortable lifestyle sought after by many. This book equips us for eternity, now.

—Bill Johnson
Author of *When Heaven Invades Earth*

ACKNOWLEDGMENTS

Mom—Thanks for loving me through hard times and always believing in me.

Bill Derryberry—Your life is an inspiration to me. Your love has brought me wholeness.

Nancy—You have helped to make my dreams come true.

Danny, Dann, Charlie, Steve, and Paul—You have helped to shape my life, my ideas, and my destiny. Thanks.

Vanessa and Allison—Thank you for the hundreds of hours that you poured into this work. This book would have never happened without your talent and support.

Bethel team—Wow! You are amazing! It is a privilege to serve with you all.

Bill and Beni—Everyone needs friends like you who will extend grace to them in hard times and see goodness in them in the dark years. I am in debt to you for the rest of my life. The two of you have altered the course of my family's history. Bill, thank you for writing this first book with me.

Earl—Although you have gone home, your life lives on through me. Thank you for adopting me. I am forever grateful for the inheritance.

Kathy—You are the woman of my dreams!

INTRODUCTION

*Paupers to Princes
The Tale of a King*

PAUPERHOOD is relegated to the children of a lesser god. It is the condition of slaves who have yet to discover their freedom on the other side of the river of baptism and find themselves still captured by the dark prince of torture and torment. He is the one who assigns them to a life of poverty, pain and depression through a diabolical play of illusion hoping to conceal their true identity forever. This evil prince feeds his captors the rations of religion to fill their soul's hunger for righteousness. These slaves, blindfolded by their sin, think that they are laboring for their own freedom and work to pave their way out of prison with bricks built from the miry clay of self-righteousness. Yet unknowingly, brick by brick, they are erecting their own chambers of death. Worse yet, these give birth to offspring of the same darkness, ultimately creating legacies of bondage with mind-sets of hopelessness.

But on a hill far away, a Lamb-turned-Lion descended into this death camp through the porthole of Golgotha. Crashing through the gates of hell, He met the dark prince in the mother of all battles. With three spikes and a thorny crown, the Captain of the Host conquered the devil, eternally disarming his destructive weapons of sin, death, hell and the grave. For sin could not tempt Him, death could not defeat Him, hell could not keep Him and the grave could not hold Him. With watching witnesses and waiting warriors, He ascended through earth's surface. The planet quaked to release its captives while Heaven thundered to receive its treasure. These were not simply rescued souls to be redeemed, but this was the crowning of the sons who were to be revealed. The Holy One of Radiance brought rotten, ragged sinners and recreated us into His righteous, reigning Saints.

We are not just soldiers of the cross; we are heirs to the throne. His divine nature permeates our souls, transforms our minds, transplants our hearts and transfigures our spirits. We were made to be vessels of His glory and vehicles of His light.

Others say the story is better reflected in the beautiful daughter who will ascend the throne through marriage, for she is betrothed to the Prince of Peace. The Bridal Chamber is beginning to be assembled, the feast is being prepared and the Bride is making herself ready. Whether we are called the Children of God, the Engaged Bride, a Royal Priesthood, the Apple of His Eye or a New Creation, one thing is for certain…we have captivated the heart of our Lover who is leading a majestic entourage, for He has mounted His white Horse and is making His way toward the planet!

Meanwhile back on earth, God's people are rising in this present darkness and beginning to shine. His Royal Army is spreading the King's glory all over the earth as we take dominion of this planet back from the defeated one. Equipped with the light of the Father, His sons are finding buried treasure in the hearts of men that was once covered by rocks of offense, thorns of treachery and relics of religion. Armed with the power of the Holy Spirit and commissioned to re-present the King's Son, we are healing the sick, raising the dead, and displacing devils. This is resulting in paupers becoming princes and the kingdom of this world becoming the Kingdom of our God!

Part I:
Our Royal Call

Chapter 1

THE PLIGHT OF PAUPERHOOD

*The earth cannot bear up under a pauper
when he becomes a king.*

I T all started on a bright summer day in the first year of the new millennium when Nancy, my personal assistant, entered my office looking rather troubled. After making small talk I decided to risk asking her what was bothering her. Nancy has a reputation for telling the truth. Her gaze penetrating my soul she said, "Sometimes you say things that hurt people's feelings. You're important to the people around you and you seem completely unaware of how much people value what you think of them. You are devastating people with your words." She went on to remind me of a comment I had made earlier. I thought I was being funny, but apparently I had actually made her my latest victim. I apologized to her, but honestly I really didn't think much of it. *After all*, I thought, *Nancy is very sensitive and I have been used to being "misunderstood" most of my life.* I went on with my day and pretty much forgot about our conversation.

That night I went to bed, fell asleep, and had a dream. In the dream a voice kept repeating this Scripture, "Under three things the earth quakes, and under four, it cannot bear up: under a pauper when he becomes a king" (Prov. 30:21-22 a). At three in the morning I woke up, feeling groggy but experiencing a deep sense of grief. I sat up against my headboard and tried to gather my thoughts.

Then I heard the Lord, who also seemed grieved, ask me, "Do you know why the earth cannot hold up under a pauper when he becomes a king?"

"No," I said, "But I have a feeling that You're going to tell me."

The Lord continued, "A pauper is born into insignificance. As he grows up he learns through life that he has no value and his opinions don't really matter. Therefore, when he becomes a king, he is important to the world around him but he still feels insignificant in the kingdom that lies within him. Subsequently, he doesn't watch his words or the way he carries himself. He ultimately destroys the very people he is called to lead. You, my son, are a pauper who has become a king."

Through the wee hours of the morning the Lord began to teach me about my identity as a prince. He took me to various Scriptures and showed me how important it is for His leaders to carry themselves as princes and princesses because we are sons and daughters of the King. The first example He showed me was Moses. He asked me, "Do you know why Moses had to be raised in Pharaoh's house?"

"No," I said.

"Moses was born to lead the Israelites out of slavery. Moses had to be raised in Pharaoh's house so that he would learn how to be a prince and not have a slave's mentality. A leader who is in slavery internally cannot free those who are in slavery externally. The first 40 years of Moses' life were just as important as the 40 years he spent in the wilderness."

When the Lord said this, it opened a door into Moses' experience for me. I began to imagine what it must have been like for him to be raised as a son of the king. He would have always known he was significant. He would have been used to people paying attention to what he said and did. He would have been accustomed to being accepted and loved. I am sure that everyone would laugh at his jokes, even when they weren't funny!

Because Moses knew he was significant, he had confidence. I saw that without that confidence he would probably have never felt empowered to do anything to help his Hebrew brothers. In fact, if he'd been raised as a slave, it might never have occurred to him to do anything about the injustice he perceived. As a prince *and* a Hebrew, the contrast between his situation and theirs created a conflict in his soul that he had to do something about. It was unjust that he was well-treated and they weren't. They were significant too.

Unfortunately, when he first tried to step in to help them, their slave mentality kept them from understanding where he was coming from. He thought they deserved to be treated like he was, but they thought he was just trying to be important when he really wasn't: "Who made you a prince?" Their mind-sets were in complete conflict.

The more I thought about the kind of person Moses must have been, the more I saw what kind of people we can be when we have been taught that we are significant and are not insecure about who we are. I also saw that I was not like Moses. As I will describe in the next chapter, I was not raised with the idea that I was significant. This caused me to develop a whole set of behaviors that someone like Moses would probably have never displayed. Even after I got saved, many of these behaviors stayed around. I saw that Nancy's confrontation was about more than her simply being sensitive and me being misunderstood, which was the way I wanted to interpret it. It was about me doing things that I've always done, but which are no longer consistent with who God says that I am.

Most importantly, I saw that if I continued to do those things, I would, as the Lord had said, ultimately destroy the people I was trying to lead. I knew this confrontation was probably one of many to come on the road out of pauperhood and into my identity as a prince. I also knew that if I didn't begin to travel that road, it would not only cost me tremendously, but also those around me.

This book shares the experiences and revelations that the Lord has used to teach me how to leave pauperhood behind and to think, act, and walk in the authority and power of my kingly and priestly call. Because this training began while I was in a position of leadership in my home church, the Lord has made it clear that what I was learning was not just to transform me, but to equip me to help promote a culture of royalty around me. This has resulted in my having the privilege of overseeing a school of ministry where the primary goal is to teach believers how to walk as princes and princesses. Before we started the school the Lord told me, "I want you to teach the students how to behave in the presence of royalty. They are called to royalty, to influence, and to rule and reign. As forerunners, I'm going to make you a people of influence."

The goal of this book is to share the revelation that the Lord has given me and that I now give to my students and the churches that I oversee. I pray that as you come along with me on this journey you will discover your own identity as a prince or princess and begin to experience all the benefits of living in the King's palace!

Chapter 2

CASTLE TRAMPS OR PALACE PRINCES

*You will always reproduce the environment around you
that you cultivate within you.*

— SUFFERING LOSS —

IN the months following my encounter with Nancy, I found out that the roots of the pauper mentality could be traced all the way back to my conception. The circumstances of my birth and my upbringing caused me to believe lies about myself that kept me from the reality of my identity in Christ.

My mother was the head high school cheerleader and my father was the star football player when they fell in love with each other. It was a storybook love affair until my mother became pregnant with me out of wedlock. It was the 1950s, a time when society attached a lot more shame to immorality than it does today. When my grandfather (my mom's father) found out that she was pregnant, he disowned both my mom and dad even though they had run away and married before I was born.

A year later, my father surprised my grandfather by coming to the back door of his house. Before my grandfather had a chance to send him away, my dad dropped to knees and begged for forgiveness. My grandfather forgave him that morning, but neither of them knew the disaster that would soon follow.

Two years later, just a year after my sister was born, my father was fishing when a huge storm suddenly came up and capsized the boat.

My father rescued my uncle, taking him to shore, and then went back to retrieve the boat. He never returned. My father drowned on that stormy night in 1958. That same night a search-and-rescue team was organized to find my dad. At around midnight, my grandfather pulled him up off the bottom of Anderson Dam. My life and the life of my family were changed forever.

My father's death created a deep sense of loss and fear of abandonment in my soul. Of course, three-year-olds don't understand what the meaning of death is. All I knew was that he was gone and I feared that my mother would be next. For many years after that, I would get up several times a night and wander into my mother's bedroom, checking to see if she was still there. She told me years later that she would often wake up and find me standing by her bed just staring at her.

— TRAGEDY TO TRASH —

My mother remarried twice. Our first stepfather came into our lives when I was five years old. He made it clear to my sister and me that he married my mother and we were just the baggage that came along with the prize. To make matters worse, he was a violent alcoholic. Brutality became a way of life for us. The house rules for survival were to "Shut up and stay out of the way." My stepfather would often say, "Children are to be seen and not heard." His point was clear: "You are not significant, no one cares about you, and no one gives a rip about what you think."

Even when we stayed out of trouble, we still never knew what kind of mood he would be in. Once, while he was drunk, he held me up by one hand, pulled my pants down, and began to beat me with his belt buckle. Blood started running down both my legs. My mother, screaming and crying, finally managed to pull me free of him.

Beyond being physically abusive, my stepfather seemed to have an agenda to rid us of all our memories of my real father. He was very jealous of my mother's love and would torment us when she showed us any affection. He destroyed all of our father's belongings and prohibited us from seeing any of our father's relatives. Looking back, I can see that the devil was using him to destroy our identities. My mother finally divorced him when I was 13 years old.

When I was 15, my mother remarried again. Miserably, the house rules remained the same. Violence continued and survival depended on all of us children becoming invisible and remaining inconspicuous.

Unfortunately I know that what I experienced growing up is all too common. The circumstances may differ, but those of us who experienced abandonment and abuse in our youth, even if it was simply being born in an "untimely manner" as I was, internalize a message that we are shameful, unwanted, and insignificant. The result of these lies is that we develop patterns of behavior that are designed to protect us in a hostile world. Because we've experienced attacks at the most fundamental levels of our identity, we think we have to do whatever it takes to kill the pain and simply survive.

One of my survival tactics was to develop a sarcastic sense of humor. My humor revolved around cutting people down and making them feel stupid and insignificant. Of course, I usually didn't realize I was making them feel bad, but subconsciously I thought that destroying other people's self-esteem helped me feel better about myself. I would joke with people about their shortcomings, thinking I was just being funny, yet every laugh cost someone a piece of their heart.

Even though I found Christ at age 18, it was many years before I dealt with my low self-esteem. As a result, my behavior continued and I still didn't have a clue how badly I was devastating people with my humor. I should have understood it, because I was the main victim of my own humor. I often made my faults the brunt of my own jokes. I had been used to feeling bad about myself for a long time. The culture of pain imprisoned my soul within me, but the Lord was determined to help me make a jail break.

— LEARNING TO LOVE YOURSELF —

When Nancy confronted me about the damage my humor was doing, I realized that it wasn't just a wake-up call to the fact that I was hurting people. The greater revelation, to me, was that people valued what I had to say. I had always believed what my stepfathers had drilled into me: People didn't really care what I thought or said. The realization that I had value began the process of uprooting the lies I believed about myself and helped me find out who I actually was. God had called me a prince, and I realized that the meeting with Nancy and the interaction I had with the Lord would just be the first of many steps that God would use to lead me out of my prison and into His palace.

I had another encounter about a year later that became the next step in my journey out of pauperhood. It began on a cold, winter Sunday evening in December. I arrived at the church late and as I opened the front door of the building, the wind nearly blew the door off its hinges. The prayer meeting was already well underway when I entered the room. About a hundred people were passionately praying so I tried to slip in quietly and not disturb the meeting. As I cleared the door, Bill, our senior leader, greeted me. He had the strangest grin on his face. He handed me something that was folded in half. I was confused by his expression as I stared at the piece of paper. I finally realized it was a check, but my disbelieving eyes struggled to communicate the amount with my brain. As it dawned on me, I began yelling, "Someone just gave me three thousand dollars! Hey everybody, someone just gave me THREE THOUSAND DOLLARS!"

Bill, laughing hysterically, said, "You'd better look at that check again!" I glanced down at the check again and realized that it was in fact written out for THIRTY THOUSAND DOLLARS! I almost passed out.

I started jumping up and down yelling, "Thirty thousand dollars! Someone just gave me THIRTY THOUSAND DOLLARS!" I was so stunned that for several minutes I could hardly talk. I looked at the signature and realized that I didn't even know the person who had given me the money. This mystery definitely thickened the plot and added to the excitement.

Many days passed before I finally discovered the benevolent man's identity. He was new to our fellowship and had attended a class that I had taught earlier in the year. One night while he was praying, he felt the Lord tell him to give me a portion of his inheritance.

I wrote him a card expressing my gratitude but the strangest thing happened next. I completely avoided him for several months after he gave me that unbelievable gift.

At first, what I was doing wasn't so obvious, yet as time went on it became more apparent. I would see him in a certain room in the church and I would turn around and walk the other direction.

On one occasion I ran to the men's restroom, wondering if I was going to make it there on time, and just as I entered the bathroom I noticed he was there. His back was turned toward me and he hadn't seen me, so I ran out. I had to run all the way to the other side of the building to find another restroom. As I was racing around the building the thought struck me, "Something is wrong with me!" I really didn't have a clue why I was behaving so strangely, and this troubled me.

When I got into bed that night, I couldn't sleep. It was cold and dark and the wind was howling. It seemed like I lay there forever. I kept looking at the clock, waiting for the day to dawn, tossing and turning and pondering why I was behaving so peculiarly. I couldn't get my poor behavior out of my head. My mind turned to other times over the years when I had the same feelings toward other people who had showed me a lot of value. I thought about how many of those relationships I had sabotaged by not allowing people to love me. I became aware that I loved to give to people, but I never liked to receive from them. Still, my behavior didn't make sense.

Finally, in desperation I sought the Lord in prayer, "Lord, do You know what is wrong with me?"

"Yes," He replied immediately.

"What is it?" I asked cautiously.

"Do you really want to know?" He asked.

This was a revealing question. I was actually fairly nervous about finding out what was wrong with me because I had lived in denial a long time. John Maxwell once said, "People change when they hurt enough they have to change, they learn enough they want to change, or they receive enough they are able to change." I recognized that I was hurting enough that I needed to change!

"Yes, I do, Lord," I replied.

Jesus said, *"The problem with you is that you don't love yourself enough to feel worthy of thirty thousand dollars. You're afraid that if that generous guy gets to know you, he'll be sorry he gave you the money. That is why you don't want him to get close to you."*

My anxiety was growing deeper. I could no longer deny that I needed help. I asked, "What should I do?"

"Learn to love yourself as much as I love you. When you do, you will expect people to love you more as they get to know you better!" He replied.

I was stunned. I could not believe what was at the root of my problem. Until this point the love I lacked for myself had never been exposed like that. I knew that others loved me (particularly my wife and kids), and I knew the Lord loved me. I didn't realize that I didn't love myself.

Through that experience I learned that whenever someone values us more than we value ourselves, we tend to sabotage our relationship with that person. Secretly, we don't want them to get close enough to find out that we aren't as good as they think we are.

From my observation as a pastor, one of the best examples of this is adult singles who are looking for a mate and can't seem to find the "right person" or someone "good enough." Many of these people have problems growing beyond friendship with the opposite sex and when the friendship starts to break the outer boundaries of their hearts, entering the inner court of their souls, they begin to do things to destroy their relationship. They are afraid that their lover will look deep within and see the imperfections they're convinced they see. It is about time we learn to love ourselves the way God loves us and see ourselves with our Father's eyes.

— NEVER ENOUGH —

There is another lie that keeps paupers from experiencing the truth of their identity in Christ. I mentioned earlier that when you are trained to feel insignificant, you develop survival skills to try to avoid the pain of that reality. A pauper uses survival skills because he believes that life is one big "dog eat dog" world. This poverty mentality is the primary attribute of a pauper. Whether a pauper has experienced poverty in his or her finances or in love and affirmation, all paupers have the common belief that there's never going to be enough for them. They live in fear, struggling with the feeling that the well is about to dry up.

God never intended for us to live in poverty in any area of our lives. The Bible is full of promises of God's provision for His people. David said, "I have been young and now I am old, yet I have not seen the righteous forsaken or his descendants begging bread" (Ps. 37:25). Jesus made it even clearer when He said,

> *Do not be worried about your life, as to what you will eat or what you will drink; nor for your body, as to what you will put on. Is not life more than food, and the body more than clothing? Look at the birds of the air, that they do not sow, nor reap nor gather into barns, and yet your heavenly Father feeds them. Are you not worth much more than they? And who of you by being worried can add a single hour to his life? And why are you worried about clothing? Observe how the lilies of the field grow; they do not toil nor do they spin, yet I say to you that not even Solomon in all his glory clothed himself like one of these. But if God so clothes the grass of the field, which is alive today and tomorrow is thrown into the furnace, will He not much more clothe you? You of little faith! Do not worry then, saying, "What will we eat?" or "What will we drink?" or "What will we wear for clothing?" For the Gentiles eagerly seek all these things; for your heavenly Father knows that you need all these things. But seek first His kingdom and His righteousness, and all these things will be added to you. So do not worry about tomorrow; for tomorrow will care for itself. Each day has enough trouble of its own* (Matthew 6:25-34).

— The Adventures of Eddie —

When my wife, Kathy, and I adopted our son Eddie, I saw firsthand how the poverty mind-set can drive people to live in a reality that tragically blinds them of the prosperity God intends to give them. Eddie grew up in physical poverty, but his attitudes and behavior typify the survival mind-set that can be seen in people who grow up in financially stable homes but experience lack in other areas of their lives.

In 1990, we started working with the Trinity County Probation Department in Lewiston, California. The Department ordered all the kids who were on probation in Lewiston to come to our youth group. Twice a week we played basketball and volleyball and then at halftime I would preach to them. Eddie was a 14-year-old young man who came every week. Eddie's mom and dad were both drug addicts so Eddie was left on his own to raise himself. He was a tall, olive-skinned, brown-haired kid. Although he wasn't on probation, he loved to play basketball with us. He hung out in the projects with the rough kids but he was usually pretty quiet. Little by little we got to know him.

About a year after we met Eddie we decided to try to adopt him. We did some research and discovered that there were two ways to gain custody. We could convince his divorced parents to sign over custody to us or we could go to court and fight for him. We decided to try to convince his parents.

I took Eddie to his mother's apartment like I had done many times before (he used to stay with us on the weekends), but this time I went to the door with him. My heart was racing and I noticed there were no lights on inside. I thought no one was home, but as Eddie forced the door open I could see a figure sitting on the floor, huddled close to the corner of the dark room. It was his mom. There was no furniture, and it was filthy beyond description. The room was freezing. I learned later that they hadn't had electricity in months.

His mother was obviously experiencing a "crash" after a drug high. She was shaking, her eyes were set in deep black circles, and her hair was matted and stringy. She looked up at me and asked, "What are you doing here?"

"I want custody of your son," I said nervously.

She glanced up at Eddie who was choking back tears, "Okay, you can have it!" she said, dropping her head in shame as she signed the custody papers.

We left Weaverville and drove to Lewiston to talk to Eddie's dad. It was quiet in the car, as my mind was flooded with images of what I had just seen. My heart was heavy and broken. I wondered how many more "Eddies" there were out there in the world. I could only hope for the best when I imagined what his father would be like.

About 30 minutes later we arrived at his dad's house. It looked like a typical drug home. The front yard was jam-packed with old cars and junk. As we approached the front door my heart raced, and I saw that the door had already been opened. Eddie went in first and I followed. As we entered the house I noticed there were several men and women sitting on the floor. A few others were lying on couches. The room was filled with smoke. A short stocky man covered with tattoos was staring at us.

He said in an angry voice, "What do you want?" I could barely find words as my heart felt like it was beating out of my chest.

"I want custody of your son," I blurted out.

He looked over at Eddie who was hanging his head and asked, "Do you want to live with him?"

"Yeah," Eddie responded.

"Fine, give me the papers and I will sign them!" He scribbled his signature in large letters and threw the papers back at me.

We left immediately. I was glad to leave there without a fistfight, and Eddie was excited to start his new life.

The next year was filled with much laughter and a lot of tears as Eddie adjusted to his new lifestyle. Little by little, we began to recognize the characteristics of a poverty mind-set in Eddie. It obviously had been formed in his heart by his grueling childhood.

We ate dinner together as a family most of the time. While we ate our meals Eddie would keep his eye on the food that was left. There was always plenty, but Eddie seemed concerned that we would run out. When the bowls would get about half full he would fill his plate again and then hide food all around his plate and in his napkin. The rest of us would just pretend we didn't notice, but it made us sad.

Eddie's first Christmas with us was exciting. We learned that he had never really had a Christmas because any gifts he received his mom would sell for drugs. We decided to go to the extreme and shower the kids with presents. We spent hundreds of dollars and distributed the money equally among all of them. There were so many gifts we could barely see the tree.

Finally Christmas Day came and we sat down together to open gifts. The whole family was having a blast watching Eddie open his gifts. He was like a little kid. The only problem was that he wouldn't let anyone hold his gifts once they were opened. Later on in the evening, after dinner, Eddie whispered something in Kathy's ear. Kathy had stockings for each of the kids and filled them with small gifts. Jason and Eddie both had comic books in their stockings. The problem was she had accidentally put four comic books in Jason's and only two in Eddie's. Eddie wanted to know why Jason got more than he got.

Eddie was always afraid he would not have enough. A poverty spirit usually leads paupers to develop a survival mentality. The fear of lack is based on lies, and until those lies are broken, people can't recognize God's provision for their lives. When Eddie became part of our family he had everything he needed and wanted. His old life was gone. But until he stopped believing those lies he couldn't relax and enjoy life with us. Thankfully, Eddie is free from his old mind-set. He has grown up to be an amazing young man and has graduated from college. (We are very proud of him.)

Paupers have a poverty mentality. They always feel like their resources are limited. They believe that when someone else receives something, it takes away some of the provision that could be theirs. They surmise that someone else's blessing costs them.

The story of the prodigal son from Luke 15 illustrates this point clearly. Having squandered his inheritance, the youngest son came home seeking refuge. His father was so excited to see him that he threw him a party. He had been saving the fattened calf for such an occasion, and finally it was time to celebrate. Everyone came to the festivity except for the elder brother; he stayed out in the field. When his father didn't see the older brother at the party, he went looking for him. He found him outside alone.

"Why aren't you coming to celebrate?" the father asked.

The older brother yelled, "You gave him the fattened calf, but you haven't even given me a goat!"

His father was stunned. He looked at his son, staring into his soul with the eyes of a loving father and said, "I gave him the fattened calf, but you own the farm" (summarized from Luke 15:11-31).

Why in the world did the older brother hang out waiting for his father to give him a goat when he owned the whole farm? He failed to recognize that he was a son and not a servant.

The revelation of our true identity will destroy the spirit of poverty in our lives. Until that happens we will keep thinking there are limits on what we get to have. As a result, we are jealous of anyone who receives something that we don't have. This leaks into all aspects of our lives including work, friends, and positions within the church.

— A KINGDOM OF FINANCES —

Unfortunately, most of us in the church are still thinking like the older brother. We have lost sight of the fact that we don't just work on the farm—we are sons and daughters of the Owner, and our Dad has plenty! I believe this revelation will totally change the way we think and plan for our futures. Most of us are still looking at our provision (what our bank statement says) to help us determine our vision, and therefore are living within *our* means instead of *His* blessings.

For example, if we are constructing a new building, we argue that we must give up some other project to cover the cost. Yet we have been called to live beyond reason and far beyond the borders of our own abilities. If we can't do any more than mere men, then let us not tell others we are a part of the church of a *living God*. We have to accomplish more than the Elk's Club if we are going to call God our Dad. This requires us to live by faith in God's provision. When we daily trust God for our substance then we *will* tap into Heaven's resources. (I know that there is a real need for true stewardship in the Body of Christ but much of what is called stewardship in the Church is simply fear that has disguised itself as wisdom.)

Paul said it best, "My God will supply all your needs according to His riches in glory in Christ Jesus" (Phil. 4:19). Did you get that? He said, "God will supply all of our needs according to *His* riches in glory!" He is not supplying according to my need but according to *His* riches.

Many times I have asked people what they do for a living. Some of them say, "I live by faith." I have learned over the years that this statement usually means, "I don't have a job. I depend on people to donate to my ministry." The unspoken belief is that people who receive a paycheck don't need to believe God for their income. This ideology is problematic. If we stop living by faith when we start receiving a regular income, then we reduce our provision down to our ability to perform instead of the Lord's ability to provide.

The pauper mentality can be found in every level of society and in all walks of life. A person's bank account is no indication whether they are experiencing the provision of God or not. Someone can have a lot of things but still feel insecure fearing something could happen to them and they'd lose it all. When paupers acquire money or things they tend to get their identity from them. The truth is that a man is not measured by what *he has* but by what *has him*. Some people own houses, but sometimes it seems that houses own people.

When we live just to get things or work so much that we don't have time for the important relationships that we have in our lives, I wonder if we own things or if they own us. The way I see it is that there is a difference between being rich and being wealthy. Wealthy people refuse to be reduced to their balance sheet and their wealth never *has* them. They don't worry about the money because they know there will always be enough. Rich people's self-esteem is attached directly to their "Profit and Loss Statement." They exert a lot of energy either chasing money or trying to keep it. I don't mean that we shouldn't have great work habits. I just mean that princes don't work for money, but rather, they work for God.

When a pauper gets a lot of money, the question that needs to be answered is, "Did God gain a fortune or lose a man?" Paupers often lose sight of their priorities when they get money, but princes don't get their identity from what they have because they know their identity is not dependent on their performance or their possessions. Princes own things, but they never let things own them. The result is that they are able to experience the worry-free life Jesus promised and are free to seek first the kingdom, knowing that all they need will be added to them.

The promised land of princehood is filled with the Father's blessings. He wants to lavish His love on us, pour out His blessings in us, and give more than we can contain. The Psalms put it best, "How blessed is the man who fears the Lord, who greatly delights in His commandments. His descendants will be mighty on earth; the generation of the upright will be blessed. Wealth and riches are in his house, and his righteousness endures forever" (Ps. 112:1-3).

Chapter 3

DUNGEONS AND DRAGONS

*Many people spend their entire lives reacting to what they don't
want to be instead of responding to the call of God on their lives.*

— POWs —

OUR past can become a prison that perpetuates the bondage of
those who raised us. Somehow we unintentionally reproduce
that same destructive culture in ourselves and in those around us. There
are a few common ways that this happens in us. One of the ways we
tether ourselves to the past is by reacting to those who abused us and
spending our lives trying not to be like them.

I have counseled a lot of people over the years and have observed
a common pattern among many of them: People typically become like
the person they most despise. Alcoholics, for instance, are commonly
raised by alcoholic parents. I personally have never met a child moles-
ter who wasn't a victim of molestation. At some point in the counseling
session, there's nearly always a statement like, "I swore I would never be
like the person who abused me, but I have become just like them." I
know this struggle well myself. In spite of struggling not to be like my
stepfathers through most of my early life, I started becoming an angry
man just like them.

During my early twenties I managed an automotive repair shop. My
temper was already growing out of control. I remember one of those
times distinctly. A customer came in to pick up his car, but we were running late and it wasn't finished. He had somewhere he needed to be so

he was a little upset. He kept coming into the shop and asking if we were done. The third time he came in, I got so mad that I grabbed a two-foot long wrench and threw it all the way across the shop at him. It was a good thing that he ducked because it barely missed his head.

Another time, I was working on a truck for several days. It was a four-wheel drive, and I had to sit inside the engine compartment to do the work. When I finally got the heads back on the engine and started it up, the problem that I thought I had fixed was still there. I was livid! I picked up a large sledgehammer and went after the truck, intending to destroy it. My boss saw me heading for the vehicle, yelling with my hammer in my hand, so he rushed over and tackled me to the ground. He held me there until I calmed down.

— WE BECOME WHAT WE IMAGINE —

I was becoming the very person I despised. One day I was reading the Old Testament and began to receive insight about my struggle through the story of Jacob and his father-in-law. Jacob was a trickster by nature. His name actually means "deceiver." He even deceived his own father out of his brother's birthright. A few chapters later, Jacob married into a family that gave him some of his own medicine. He worked for his father-in-law, Laban, for seven years so he could marry Laban's daughter Rachel. When he woke up on the honeymoon morning, Leah was in his bed. Laban had neglected to tell him that their family tradition dictated that the oldest daughter marry first. He finagled another seven years of work out of Jacob with this trick because Jacob still wanted Rachel. Thankfully he got her on credit! He received her a week later and then paid for her in small monthly installments over the next seven years.

After 14 years of mistrust and dishonesty, Jacob was ready to leave. He told his father-in-law to give him what was his so he could go his own way. Laban was no fool. He knew that Jacob was making him a fortune. Laban told Jacob to name his wage and stay with him. Jacob knew that no matter what his wages were, his father-in-law would find some way to cheat him out of it. He said, "You have changed my wage ten times!" Jacob told Laban that he would work for all the spotted and speckled sheep and goats. These animals would become his wage. They struck a deal.

I am sure Laban thought that he got to Jacob again as there were probably very few spotted and speckled among the flocks. But the story takes on the most unusual twist. Jacob carved branches, exposing the white beneath the bark. He then put the branches in front of the watering troughs whenever the best of the sheep were drinking and mating there. This resulted in the strongest sheep and goats giving birth to spotted and speckled offspring. Before long, Jacob became rich because his flocks prospered while Laban's flocks were feeble.

As I pondered this unusual passage, it dawned on me that this was not a lesson in agriculture! God was demonstrating how we, *His* sheep, reproduce. The watering hole is a place of *reflection*, which means both gazing at something and meditating on it. Meditation involves our imagination. If we feed our imagination with thoughts of what we don't want to become and drink from the well of regret, we reproduce that very thing in ourselves. It doesn't matter *what we want to reproduce*. It's only important *what we imagine* while we are thinking and drinking at the watering hole of our imagination.

This principle is also illustrated in the creation of man. The Bible says we were created in God's image. In other words, what God *imagined*, we became. Proverbs says, "For as a man thinks in his heart, so is he" (Prov. 23:7). Our imagination is a very powerful part of our being. Everything that has ever been built, made, painted, or developed began in someone's imagination. We tend to reproduce what we feast our thoughts upon.

What I am realizing about many of us is that we spend much of our lives reacting to what we don't want to be instead of responding to the call of God on our lives. We waste a lot of energy trying *not* to be something. In order to not be something, I have to keep it in front of me so I can avoid it. The crazy thing is that I reproduce what I imagine. If I see what I don't want to be, just envisioning it causes me to reproduce it. This explains why so many people grow up mistreating their children in the same way that their parents abused them. They promised themselves that they would never become like their folks, but they became just like them.

— REACTING TO THE PAST OR RESPONDING TO THE VISION —

We break out of this prison by responding to the call of God on our lives and meditating on His vision for us. The word *meditation* is related to the word *medicine*. In a positive sense, meditation means to "think in such a way as to make oneself healthy." We become the person He has called us to be when we meditate on the things of God and dream His dreams. The Psalmist wrote, "Delight yourself in the Lord, and He will give you the desires of your heart" (Ps. 37:4). Bill Johnson has a creative definition of *desire*. He breaks it down into two parts: "de" meaning "of," and "sire" meaning "to father." When we delight ourselves in God, instead of hanging out in our past, He becomes the father, the sire, of our dreams.

Mary illustrates this principle in her life. The Bible says, "But Mary treasured all these things, pondering them in her heart" (Luke 2:19). She pondered the word of God in her heart and gave birth to the Savior of the world. What she imagined became flesh and dwelt among us through immaculate conception. When we dream with God, *we* become the masterpieces of *His* imagination.

— BOUND BY UNFORGIVENESS —

Another thing that ties us to the past is unforgiveness. Unforgiveness causes us to waste our lives trying to get even instead of fulfilling our own destiny by walking in our call. It is important that we forgive all those who sinned against us so we can be free to go on with our lives. It is also crucial that we learn to forgive ourselves for our own sins.

Many people spend their lives hating others and planning for revenge. Bitterness has no friends. There is no container known to man that will hold it. It always leaks out onto those we love the most.

It is the privilege and the responsibility of royalty to forgive. Solomon, who was raised to be a prince from birth said, "A man's discretion makes him slow to anger, and it is his glory to overlook a transgression" (Prov. 19:11). After Jesus rose from the dead, He breathed on His disciples, releasing His Spirit into them. Then He gave them their first mission as Spirit-filled believers, "If you forgive the sins of any, their sins have been forgiven them; if you retain the sins of any, they have been retained" (John 20:23).

I received the Lord in 1973 during the "Jesus Movement." I was 18 years old and living with a ton of pain in my heart. I used to lie in bed at night imagining creative ways to destroy the people who had abused me. I didn't just want them dead; I wanted them to suffer the way they had caused me to suffer. Soon after I got saved, the Lord began to confront my unforgiveness. He told me that I needed to forgive the people who abused me or I would open the door to the tormentors in my life. It wasn't easy at first but I realized that He had given me the power to forgive when He forgave me.

— Unforgiveness Invites Tormentors —

The Lord's warning to me about "the tormentors" became clear when I read an interesting story that Jesus told about *our* King and *our* Kingdom. He was responding to Peter's question about how many times he had to forgive. (It still seems humorous to me that Peter is the one asking Jesus how many times he has to forgive when he is the most offensive guy on the team.) Jesus said:

> *For this reason the kingdom of heaven may be compared to a king who wished to settle accounts with his slaves. When he had begun to settle them, one who owed him ten thousand talents was brought to him. But since he did not have the means to repay, his lord commanded him*

to be sold, along with his wife and children and all that he had, and repayment to be made.

So the slave fell to the ground and prostrated himself before him, saying, "Have patience with me and I will repay you everything." And the lord of that slave felt compassion and released him and forgave him the debt.

But that slave went out and found one of his fellow slaves who owed him a hundred denarii; and he seized him and began to choke him, saying, "Pay back what you owe."

*So his fellow slave fell to the ground and began to plead with him, saying, "Have patience with me and I will repay you." But he was unwilling and went and threw him in prison until he should pay back what was owed. So when his fellow slaves saw what had happened, they were deeply grieved and came and reported to their lord all that had happened. Then summoning him, his lord said to him, "You wicked slave, I forgave you all that debt because you pleaded with me. Should you not also have had mercy on your fellow slave, in the same way that I had mercy on you?" And his lord, moved with anger, **handed him over to the torturers until he should repay all that was owed him. My heavenly Father will also do the same to you, if each of you does not forgive his brother from your heart** (Matthew 18:23-35).*

This story is stunning to me. Unforgiveness puts us in prison. If we fail to understand how big our debt of sin was to God and what it meant for Him to forgive it, we can fall into the trap of judging the much smaller wrongs of those around us. As we can see from the story, we are only hurting ourselves when we do that. God insists that His people forgive each other, and He's not above using the devil as a pawn to help us do it. This parable describes His "ways and means committee" called "the tormentors" that help drive us into forgiveness.

— Captives and Prisoners —

Isaiah said that we were anointed to proclaim "liberty to captives" and "freedom to prisoners" (Isa. 61:1). I believe he is describing two kinds of people behind bars: "captives" and "prisoners." Prisoners are people whom the judge sends to prison. It takes a court order from the Judge of Heaven to release them. These folks have opened the door of their life to the tormentors through sin and unforgiveness. They must forgive those who have hurt and abused them in order for God, who is the ultimate judge, to be justified in calling off the tormentors and releasing them from prison.

Over the years this truth has been reemphasized to me as I work with people who are tormented by demons. I remember one of those times so clearly. Randy Clark came to Redding for a conference. He was preaching about freedom one night and in the middle of his message he commanded the demonic spirits to leave people who were present. Several people started screaming and falling to the floor.

One lady in her mid-forties was in the front of the church. She began to act crazily. The ministry team was trying to take her into a room to pray for her, but when they got her into the hallway leading to the prayer room she began to act like an animal. She started biting and clawing and beating her head against the wall while she snarled at people. The team gathered around her and started yelling at the spirits to leave her alone, but made no progress at all. When I arrived to help, she was screaming and clawing while they yelled back at her. If the futility of their attempts to help wasn't so sad, it may have looked comical.

I asked, "What are you guys doing?"

"We are getting this lady delivered! What does it look like we are doing?" one of them said in a sarcastic tone.

"It looks like the devil is winning!" I fired back. (There are a lot of people who need to get delivered from their last deliverance.)

"If you think you can do better, you can do it yourself," another responded in frustration.

I moved into the circle and put my arms around her to keep her from beating her head against the wall. I whispered in her ear asking her if there was anyone she needed to forgive.

She yelled, "No!" Then the Lord showed me a picture of her father raping her, so I asked her if she needed to forgive her father. She started screaming, "I hate him! I hate his guts! He can rot in hell!"

I said, "If you don't want to forgive him, then I can't help you. The demons have permission to torment you." I got up and started to walk away.

When I got to the door, she (still going crazy) yelled down the hall, "Fine, I'll forgive him! I'll do anything! Just help me!" A few minutes later I led her in a prayer of forgiveness for her dad and some other people who came to mind. Then we commanded the demons to leave. They left and she got up laughing!

Forgiveness doesn't mean I ever have to trust the person who abused me. It simply means that I release them from being punished for what they did to me. If a man rapes a woman, she may never trust him again, but she has to forgive him or the tormentors will torment her.

— FORGIVENESS RESTORES THE STANDARD —

Forgiveness also restores the standard in our lives. I remember one time when our kids were all teenagers. I became angry with Kathy in front of them and then treated her disrespectfully. The next day I gathered the kids together in the front room and asked Kathy and each of the kids to forgive me. They all did, and we went on with our day. About a week later one of our boys came in the kitchen and started being sarcastic with Kathy. I walked in and told him that he didn't have permission to talk to my wife like that.

He said, "You were rude to Mom the other day yourself!"

I said, "Yes, but you forgave me. Forgiveness restores the standard. When you forgave me, you gave away your right to act that same way because your forgiveness restored me back to the place of honor. I repented. Repentance means, "to be restored to the pinnacle, the high place."

He told his mother that he was sorry and she forgave him. If we don't understand this principle, then the lowest point, the worst mistake, or the stupidest thing we have ever done in life becomes our high watermark. For instance, if we were immoral as a teenager and later on in life we have teenagers ourselves, we won't have confidence to correct them for their poor sexual choices because we failed ourselves. Failures we have repented of are no longer the standard that we must bow to. When we asked God and those we have hurt to forgive us, we were set back up to the high place God assigned to us. Otherwise the worst day of our life becomes the highest place that we have the right to lead others to. The truth is that forgiveness restores the standard of holiness in us and through us.

— ANOTHER PRISON DOOR —

Jealousy, envy, and fear can also lead us out of our destiny and into the dungeon. The story of Saul and David returning home from their great victory over Goliath and his army is a perfect example of this. It reads:

> *The women sang as they played, and said, "Saul has slain his thousands, and David his ten thousands."*
>
> *Then Saul became very angry, for this saying displeased him; and he said, "They have ascribed to David ten thousands, but to me they have ascribed thousands. Now what more can he have but the kingdom?" Saul looked at David with suspicion from that day on. Now it came about on the next day that **an evil spirit from God came mightily upon Saul**, and he raved in the midst of the house, while David was playing the harp with his hand, as usual; and a spear was in Saul's hand* (1 Samuel 18:7-10).

Notice that the Lord sent the evil spirit on Saul. This is much like the story Jesus told in Matthew 18 about the tormentors who drive us into forgiveness. They can also drive us out of the land of jealousy. Saul's life is an example of how jealousy blinds us to reality and leads us to irrational conclusions. Saul thought that David would overthrow him as king simply because he was more capable. He didn't understand that God's Kingdom is not a performance-based kingdom. We don't lead because we are necessarily the most qualified; we lead because we are "called" to be the leader.

Princes and princesses are commissioned to see the people they lead reach their full potential in God. This means that the greatest compliment we can ever have is when the people we are leading become greater than us. If we believe that we are leading because we are the most qualified, then we will subconsciously work to undermine other people's advancements.

The life of King Saul also shows us how suspicion can masquerade as discernment and ultimately lead us into bondage. Suspicion is the gift of discernment being used by the spirit of fear. It leads to bitterness, unforgiveness, and torment, and it results in our going into a spiritual prison where all guards work for the dark side. The spirits who guard the walls of this prison have names like sickness, depression, hatred, and murder.

— LIBERTY TO CAPTIVES —

Isaiah also said that there were people who were "captives." Captives are people who have been captured in battle and held as prisoners of war. These people do not have unforgiveness in their hearts, but instead are bound by the lies they have believed. Jesus said, "You will know the truth, and the truth will make you free" (John 8:32). The word *truth* here means "reality." So many of us live in a "virtual reality"; it feels real and looks real, but it isn't real. It is just an illusion. We give the devil permission to punish us because we think his lies are true. When we are tormented because of lies we need a revelation of the truth of God so we can escape to freedom.

This testimony will make my point clearer. One day I was teaching upstairs in the School of Ministry and about halfway through my sermon someone came running up to me with an urgent message. We ran downstairs together, finally arriving at our counselor's office. About eight people were fervently praying outside the room. I opened up the office door to a wild scene. A very large woman was on the floor facedown with one of our strongest maintenance workers on top of her, trying to restrain her. Two of our counselors were standing up against the wall with the lady's arms wrapped around their legs. She was biting their shoes and growling at them.

The first question in my mind was, "Why do the demons have permission to torment this woman? Was she a prisoner who had sin and/or unforgiveness issues in her life, or was she a captive who believed a lie?" I got on the floor and began to ask the Holy Spirit for insight into her bondage.

Suddenly I heard Him say, "When she was a little girl she was told that she blasphemed the Holy Spirit and was therefore banished to hell." The Spirit continued, "It's a lie. I have forgiven her."

I leaned over and whispered in her ear, "The devil told you when you were a little girl that you blasphemed the Holy Spirit, but it's a lie! You never did that. Renounce that lie." She immediately calmed down and began to laugh. Within seconds she was completely delivered. Knowing the truth will make you free!

We must leave the prison behind to come into the palace. People of royalty focus on who they are called to be. They have forgiven those who have hurt them, they have rejected the lies of the enemy, and they have embraced the truth. They don't live in the bondage of prison but in the wholeness of the palace. Let our journey as royalty begin!

Chapter 4

A ROYAL FLUSH

(BY BILL JOHNSON)

Forgiveness rewrites our history!

— WHEN GOD'S ROYALTY TOUCHES OUR PAST —

WHENEVER we review the events of our lives apart from the blood of Jesus, we subject ourselves to the influence of the spirit of deception. In reality, my sinful past no longer exists. The Lamb of God purchased it with a payment in blood, forever removing my sins from the records of Heaven. The atoning blood of Jesus covers my sin, never to be uncovered again. Sin's power to destroy us is itself destroyed by a superior reality: forgiveness.

The devil keeps records of our past. Yet those records are powerless without our agreement. He is the *accuser of the brethren*, but Jesus is our defender. We make an agreement with the accuser whenever we look at our past apart from the blood. When we agree with the devil, we empower him. When he is empowered, he devours.

On the other hand, agreeing with God empowers us. It frees us from the power of a lie and enables us to live according to the will of God. This empowerment is not independent of God; it is empowerment *because* of God. When we agree with God we step into the power of truth, the momentum of the Cross. The truth is already in our favor because King Jesus died in our place. He not only died *for* us, He died *as* us. Our agreement with God, which is always the focus and activity of faith, enables us to reap the fruit of truth. And that fruit is freedom! Faith grows by agreeing with God from the heart.

— THE PATHWAY TO HUMILITY —

Religion rubs our noses in the past to keep us humble. Reviewing the sinfulness of our past in order to become humble is a perversion. It actually creates shame; and shame is a poor counterfeit of humility. Shame is the fruit of humiliation that works against the truth. To maintain consciousness of our sinful past to help us become more humble is the cruelty of a religious spirit; it requires us to keep something in our minds that isn't in God's. In reality, it is much more humbling to live in the liberty of unearned forgiveness. When we are forgiven, the King gives us permission to live as though we had never sinned.

Living in forgiveness does not mean we are to forget our past. Rather, seeing my past through the blood of Jesus brings praise to my lips and frees me from the burden of a guilty heart. Jesus will be known throughout eternity as the Lamb of God; so we will always remember that it was the provision of the spotless Lamb that obtained eternal redemption for us.

— MY PERSONAL STORY —

I struggled for so many years with this truth. Shame and discouragement were close friends of mine. I would counter such feelings with more prayer, study, and reading about the lives of great men and women of God from the past. Yet my problem wasn't solved, even though I was doing what most would counsel me to do. I found that when our perspective is wrong, more study and prayer can actually add to our discouragement and shame, as it did for me. Every biography impressed me, but also made me feel hopeless. They were all too perfect. I couldn't relate to any of their God-encounters. It seemed that they were God's favorites, and I just existed. One day I heard a tape from David Wilkerson called, "Facing Your Failures." In it he talked about how the "great ones" all had failures and weaknesses, too. He shared some of his struggles and failures. It was the most refreshing message I had heard in my life. It was the beginning of a change in perspective for me. But the religious spirit was not about to give up on me so easily.

I had surrounded myself with people of like passion—revival at any cost! I was weaned on this theme. I slept, ate, and prayed it constantly. But it was common knowledge to all of us who had studied the revivals of the past—*we weren't holy enough*. So I constantly re-examined my motives and personal holiness, and always came up short. My passion for God was alive and well, but my efforts at personal holiness were killing me. I am embarrassed to admit it, but I was a pastor for a few years before I actually started to get well. Every week I would get buried in my stuff—my sense of worthlessness and hopelessness. Thankfully, I was able to "faith my way out of it" by Sunday so I could give the people I pastored something healthy to eat.

A dear friend and mentor of mine, Darol Blunt, lived a life of grace. Life seemed so easy for him. He walked me through so much and modeled a life without the intense introspection that I was trapped in. He laughed a lot, and knew how to have fun without being coarse. That was new to me. I was too serious for my own good. I had been a class clown while growing up, and had learned how to be crude for effect. I turned from this and everything else I knew to follow God completely. Unfortunately, I left a valuable part of who I was back on the chopping block of personal holiness, and picked up a false image of spirituality that never did work.

How did God begin to change me? There wasn't a one-moment encounter that changed everything. But there was a series of things that God brought my way to establish me in Him and break off the religious spirit that had me bound. Repentance was needed. It sounds strange to say it, because repentance was a major theme of mine. Yet true repentance is to "change the way we think." I needed repentance that would affect my mind, and redirect my heart toward a God who forgives. Faith is evidence of true repentance. I wasn't living in secret sin. There were no unrighteous habits in my life to torment my conscience with shame. My shame was over my humanity, and my discouragement was over who I wasn't. At some point I actually had to believe that what King

Jesus did was enough. It sounds so simple now. My shame quietly denied His atoning work. My discouragement dishonored the sufficiency of the King's promises.

— I DON'T DO INTROSPECTION —

It took a while, but I finally realized that my best moments (mentally, emotionally, and spiritually) were when I just did my best, and stayed away from introspection. This was a scary thing for me, because in my mind introspection was almost a rite of passage to my biggest dream—to be a revivalist. After years of struggling with the conflict of personal holiness, I prayed something like this:

> *Father,*
>
> *You know that I don't do so well when I look inward, so I'm going to stop. I am relying on You to point out to me the things that I need to see. I promise to stay in Your Word. You said that Your Word was a sword—so please use it to cut me deeply. Expose those things in me that are not pleasing to You. But in doing so, please give me the grace to forsake them. I also promise to come before You daily. Your presence is like a fire. Please burn from me those things that are unpleasing to You. Melt my heart until it becomes like the heart of Jesus. Be merciful to me in these things. I also promise to stay in fellowship with Your people. You said that iron sharpens iron. I expect You to anoint the "wounds of a friend" to bring me to my senses when I'm being resistant toward You. Please use these tools to shape my life until Jesus alone is seen in me. I believe that You have given me Your heart and mind. By Your grace I am a new creation. I want that reality to be seen that the name of Jesus would be held in highest honor.*

— REVISING HISTORY —

Forgiveness, in effect, changes the past. God's journal records our life from the perspective of His forgiveness and our faith. His Book of

Remembrance doesn't contain our history of sin and stupidity. Consider Sarah, Abraham's wife. In Genesis 18 (NKJV) she, "laughed within herself saying, 'After I have grown old, shall I have pleasure my Lord, being old also?'"

And the Lord said to Abraham, "Why did Sarah laugh? Saying, 'Shall I bear a child since I am old?' Is anything too hard for the Lord? At the appointed time, I will return to you, according to the time of life and Sarah shall have a son."

But Sarah denied it, saying, "I did not laugh." For she was afraid.

And He said, "No, you did laugh."

The Hebrew word for *laughter* in this verse tells us that she didn't give a sheepish chuckle. She actually mocked God and what He had said, and then made matters worse by lying to the Lord about doing so. But Hebrews 11:11 (NKJV) says, "By faith, Sarah herself also received strength to conceive seed and she bore a child when she was past the age because she judged Him faithful who had promised."

This is the same woman! What happened? Apparently she repented, turning her heart to what God had declared to be her destiny. In doing so God rewrote her history, excluding the sin that is recorded in Scripture. What's written in Hebrews 11 shows us how God records our life's events in His Book of Remembrance. God wrote her story in such a way as to emphasize what pleases Him the most—her faith. It seems as if He is boasting all over Heaven about Sarah, "Did you see that courage and that great faith? Here's a lady—she can't bear a child, but she knows that I'm faithful!" You can see Him talking to the Scribe angel, "Make sure you put it like this…'That's my girl! She believed me—others wouldn't have, but she did!'"

When God views a believer's history like that, who are we to do otherwise? The blood actually changes our history into His story. Some years ago I heard a prophetic word that really touched my heart. In it, God spoke saying, "I will not remove the scars from your life. Instead I will rearrange them in such a way that they have the appearance of carving on a fine piece of crystal." Such is the love of God. What was despised becomes a testimony of God's grace—a thing of beauty!

— HOW WE THINK —

The mind set on the flesh is death and at war with God. That is the "unrenewed" mind. In essence, the renewed mind is the mind of Christ. It is able to demonstrate the will of God, which is best described in the prayer, "Thy will be done, on earth as it is in heaven"(Matt. 6:10). The exhortation of Scripture is clear, "Let this mind be in you which was also in Christ Jesus" (Phil. 2:5 NKJV). The renewing of the mind begins with our new identity obtained at the cross. We were once slaves of sin, but are now slaves of righteousness. Our thought life must support that reality. The apostle Paul emphasized this in his letter to the church at Rome, saying, "Even so, think of yourself dead to sin" (Rom. 6:11). It's an attitude…a way of thinking…an evidence of repentance.

The mind has a power to affect our behavior either positive or negatively. But it does not possess the power to change our nature. That alone is accomplished when we are born again. When people are born again, they are transformed from the inside out. It is not the external things that are likely to change first. God takes up residence in our hearts, transforming us, as it really is *an inside job*. On the other hand, religion works on the outside. While it can bring conformity, it is powerless to bring transformation.

"For as he thinks within himself, so he is" (Prov. 23:7). When we are charged to think of ourselves *dead to sin*, it is more than a suggestion to think positively about our conversion. It is an invitation to step into the momentum of a reality made available only through the cross. The supernatural power released in this way of thinking is what creates a lifestyle of freedom. It is able to do this because it is TRUTH. To say that I have sinned is true. To say I am free of sin is truer still. The renewed mind is necessary to more consistently taste the supernatural life, which God intended to be the normal Christian life.

— How God Thinks About Us —

Just as the kings of the Old Testament needed the prophets, so the royal priesthood of this hour needs servants of the Lord to help complete the picture of God's purposes in our lives. I appreciate the many times members of the Body of Christ have given me an encouraging word that God has placed on their hearts. This is the essence of the prophetic ministry. The Holy Spirit is quick to confirm when something is actually from Him. When it is, I treasure it greatly. I write them out so I can review them whenever necessary. Most of them are on index cards that are in my briefcase all the time. Some of those words go back 20 years or more, and they still bring life to me. I can't afford to think differently about my life than God does. Whether it's a Scripture promise that God has highlighted for my life, or a prophetic word from a recognized prophet, I review them until what is said is what I think.

Promises are like the rudder of a ship. Rudders determine the direction of that ship. And what I do with God's promises determine the direction of my thought-life, and eventually affect my reality. It is essential to understand what God thinks of me (and others) in order to step into my destiny. Regardless of circumstances, God's word is true. "Let God be found true, though every man be found a liar" (Rom. 3:4). Again, we cannot afford to think differently about ourselves than God does.

I love to meditate on the Scriptures that speak of what Jesus accomplished for me through salvation. Below are several verses that I have found to bring me nourishment:

> *For as high as the heavens are above the earth, so great is His lovingkindness toward those who fear Him. As far as the east is from the west, so far has He removed our transgressions from us* (Psalm 103:11-12).

> *"They will not teach again, each man his neighbor and each man his brother, saying, 'Know the Lord,' for they will all know Me, from the least of them to the greatest of them," declares the Lord, "For I will forgive their iniquity, and their sin I will remember no more"* (Jeremiah 31:34).

For I will pour out water on the thirsty land and streams on the dry ground; I will pour out My Spirit on your offspring and My blessing on your descendants; and they will spring up among the grass like poplars by streams of water. This one will say, "I am the Lord's"; and that one will call on the name of Jacob; and another will write on his hand, "Belonging to the Lord," and will name Israel's name with honor (Isaiah 44:3-5).

Being confident of this very thing, that He who has begun a good work in you will complete it until the day of Jesus Christ (Philippians 1:6 NKJV).

My Father, who has given them to Me, is greater than all; and no one is able to snatch them out of the Father's hand (John 10:29).

Therefore if anyone is in Christ, he is a new creature; the old things passed away; behold, new things have come (2 Corinthians 5:17).

These are just a few of the thoughts that God has toward us that must become a part of what and how we think. Make your own list, and change your mind.

— THE BEST KEPT SECRET —

"God will not share His glory with another" (Isa. 42:8). The most common understanding of this verse is that God is glorious and we are not. In reality we are not "another." Why do you think He made us individual members of His body? The lowest (the least) member of His body is superior to the highest principality and power of darkness. The original target in the creation of man was for us to live and dwell in His glory. "All have sinned and fall short of the glory of God" (Rom. 3:23). The cross removes the obstacle to His purposes, and restores us to His original intent. The religious heart is unwilling to recognize that we really have been made in His image, and that being born again restores us to a place of absolute purity.

Jesus added to this in His priestly prayer, "The glory which You have given Me I have given to them, that they may be one, just as We are one" (John 17:22). It is recorded in Proverbs that wisdom will bring to us a crown of glory. Even our bodies were designed to live in His glory. As we become more and more accustomed to the presence of His glory, even our bodies *hunger for* God's glorious presence. The sons of Korah, who had spent considerable time in the actual glory of God, and had seen the effect on their physical being, sang, "My heart and my flesh cry out for the living God" (Ps. 84:2 NKJV).

When God's royalty touches our lives, we discover we are designed to live in God's glory. We no longer live in the bondages of our past—performance and comparison in our daily lives, but we know our worth in simply loving Him. For out of that springs living water and revelation for those who have not found the truth in the nations of the earth!

— BIBLIOGRAPHY —

Hebrews 6:1b, *"Repentance from dead works and of faith toward God."*

NAS—Repentance and faith are two sides of the same coin. To move *from* something automatically means you have to move *toward* something.

Chapter 5

LIZARDS IN THE PALACE

Whatever you misdiagnose you will mistreat.

— WHAT'S YOUR NAME? —

KATHY and I took two of our grandchildren to Marine World some time ago. Elijah, who was three at the time, and his cousin Mesha, who was five, were in the hotel room with us, sitting on the bed.

They were watching a National Geographic documentary about reptiles on television. When it was over, Mesha looked at Elijah and said, "Let's play crocodiles and lizards!"

Elijah, although he is younger, is much stronger than Mesha. He said, "Yeah!"

Mesha said, "I am the crocodile and you are the lizard."

"Ok," Elijah said excitedly.

Suddenly they both stood up on the bed and began to wrestle. Within a minute, Elijah had Mesha pinned down on the mattress.

"You can't do that, Elijah!" Mesha complained. "You are the lizard. I am the crocodile!"

At her protest, he immediately let her up. "What do lizards do?" he asked.

"They lick things with their tongues like this." She demonstrated by licking his cheek.

"Okay," Elijah said submissively.

A few seconds later, she had convinced him to lie down so she could get on top of him. "Raaaaw! Raaaaw!" Mesha roared as she struggled to hold him down.

Every time Elijah started to push her off, she would say, "Elijah, you are a lizard. I am a crocodile! You can't do that. You can only use your tongue."

Finally, after about ten minutes, a little voice came out from under Mesha, "Papa, I don't want to play anymore."

This story reminds me so much of the game of life. The devil gives us names that disempower us. We become the lizards who can only use our tongues. He becomes the powerful crocodile. Then we spend our lives playing by his rules because we believe in the wrong name.

The devil is the accuser, and he often uses other people to propagate his alias identities over us. My first stepfather used to call me a "stupid ass" all the time. This resulted in me always feeling dumb, which really hindered my ability to learn. The name became a mental block, which manifested as a difficulty with reading. When I finished high school I only read at a third grade level.

I have met many women who were called "whores" by their fathers, then struggled with immorality their entire lives. Names can be prophetic declarations that define a person's identity. Because people act according to who they believe they are, these lies are ultimately acted out in their behavior.

We respond to our environment according to the way we see ourselves. Words spoken to us become names that we carry in our hearts. These names paint a portrait of us in our imagination and become the lenses through which we view our world. *Sticks and stones are breaking our bones, but names are taking away our future!*

— Names Are Prophetic Declarations —

Just as bad names can hold people in bondage and lead them into destruction, great names can release power into our lives and bring us into our God-given destinies. Many people in the Bible were insignifi-cant until their names were changed. Simon wasn't an apostle until he was named Peter. Saul was not an apostle until his name was changed to Paul.

It is so important that we live by our God-given names and not by names that tie us to bondage. We must break free of all aliases that we have been given by the world. Jacob understood this principle well. In Genesis 32, we find Jacob at a river called "Jabbok," which means "empty and alone." His brother is after him, his wives are always arguing with each other and his father-in-law is mad at him. Like many of us, I'm sure Jacob realized that he was a big part of the problem, but he probably felt powerless to change himself. Jacob was compelled to deceive because, as I mentioned in the last chapter, his name meant "trickster." He was reminded of his shortcomings every time people would call him by his name. We will always act out of who we believe we are: Jacob deceived because his name was deceiver. His behavior eventually creat-ed a culture of deception around him, and consequently his wives also became liars and deceivers.

Suddenly, at the lowest part of Jacob's life, he encounters an angel. (You know you're having a tough life when even the angel sent to bless you doesn't like you!) He wrestles with him all night long. The angel mangles him, but Jacob refuses to let the angel go until he blesses him. The angel argues that his shift is over because it is morning and he has to leave. But Jacob persists.

Finally the angel asks him, "What is your name?"

He responds, "My name is Jacob."

The angel continues, "Your name shall no longer be Jacob, but Israel; for you have striven with God and with men and have prevailed" (Gen. 32:24-28).

Can you imagine fighting with an angel all night long, getting thrashed, and letting him go just because he called you by a nickname? If you wrestled with an angel for one wish, wouldn't you ask him for a new house, a car, or something of monetary significance? Would you let him go just for a name change? You would if you understood the reve-lation Jacob had. His new name, "Israel," meant "a prince of God." The name released him into his prophetic destiny. It is no accident that after his name was changed, he became the father of one of the greatest nations in the world.

A prophetic declaration is more than mere words, because it releas-es grace to accomplish what it says. Names in the Bible were given to people as a prophetic declaration of their identity and actually released the very characteristics of their calling to them. Grace as well as dis-grace is released by name-calling. Grace is the "operational power of God." Grace is the God-given ability to become what you couldn't become before you received the declaration. Disgrace also has the power to release curses from the dark side.

In the Book of Genesis, God invited Adam to create with Him by naming the animals. When Adam named the animals he was prophesy-ing their DNA and what they were to become in the world, not just call-ing them a normal animal name like "Fifi" or "Spot!"

The power of a declared name is also illustrated in the third chap-ter of Genesis. Here Adam named his wife "Eve." Eve means "mother of the living." She was barren until her name was changed from "Woman" to "Eve." After Adam's prophetic declaration, Eve gave birth to Cain and Abel.

Once we realize who we are, our behavior changes because we always act out of our "self-understood" identity. Abram had to have a name change to fulfill his call. God prophesied to Abram that he was going to be the father of many nations. Before he could come into his destiny, his name had to be changed from Abram, which means "exalted father," to Abraham, "the father of a multitude." His name had been limit-ing his destiny!

When the Lord met me and told me I was a pauper who had become a prince, He was giving me a name change. Once I knew my new name, I had access to the grace I needed to begin walking in a new identity. It is vital that we all hear the name the Lord has given to us and allow that name to define our identities. When we get to Heaven, we will be given a new name written on a white stone that only we will know. This name will be birthed from a foundation of purity (white stone) and intimacy (no one will know it but you and Jesus). We will need a new identity that is congruent with our new calling (see Rev. 2:17).

— ACTING OUT OF OUR IDENTITY —

It seems to me that our whole society is having a major identity crisis. Most people have no clue who they are or what they are supposed to be doing with their lives. The way we raise our children in America perpetuates the crisis.

When children first learn to talk they ask, "What's that?" a thousand times a day.

Next comes the famous, "Why?"

Kathy and I have seven grandchildren below the age of seven years. My conversations with my grandchildren go something like this:

"Papa what is that?"

"It is a ball," I answer.

"Why Papa?"

"So we can have fun," I reply.

"Why Papa?"

"So we won't be bored," I tell them.

"Why Papa?"

Finally I send them to Grandma so they can ask her the same questions all over again. When our children hit puberty they start asking another question, *"Who am I?"* The struggle in our society is that we don't have an answer for that question so we send them off to college to learn *how to do* something, thinking that if they learn enough it will satisfy their longing for identity. Identity doesn't come from education but from impartation. We can't educate ourselves into our identities. Proper identity comes from the impartation of our heavenly Father speaking to us through the people He has assigned to give oversight to us.

You have to be a human being before you are a human doing. When we try to "do" something without first "being" someone, we usually find ourselves making a living at a job we hate. Another ramification of this failure to discover true identity is that many people learn to derive their self-esteem from what they *do*. This may seem fine for a while if they can perform well. When they can't perform anymore, for whatever reason, their self-esteem goes into the pit.

This point was driven home to me a while back when I took a long plane trip to the South Pacific. I sat next to a young college student. We had an 11-hour flight together and we seemed to have nothing in common. After a couple of hours I decided to try to get some sleep. When I closed my eyes I had a thought about the young man sitting next to me.

I turned to him and asked, "What do you want to do with your life?"

"I want to be an attorney," he replied.

I found myself saying, "You'll be a lousy attorney!"

He perked up and in an angry voice snapped back, "What do you mean by that?"

I said, "Attorneys have an extremely high value for justice. They need justice so badly that they will violate their relationships to get it. You have a really great value for relationships. You need to be validated, loved and nurtured. Your need for justice is low on your priority list. The first time you get into court and have to attack someone's character to make your case, you're not going to sleep at night."

"That is exactly right!" he said.

"You know what you need to do?"

"No, what?" he replied.

"You have amazing gift mix. You have a very creative side that expresses itself in something like acting. You also have an extremely left-brained side that likes to organize things and administrate them. I see your bedroom being really organized and the clothes in your closet hanging in the order of color. You would be a great movie director if you would give yourself to that."

He almost jumped out of his seat. He said excitedly, "I do organize my room and my clothes just like you described. I have always wanted to be a director and I was the head of my drama class in high school!"

"That's what you need to do with your life," I told him. "You are the next Steven Spielberg!"

Many of us spend our lives doing something that is different from who we are. When our activities are an expression of our person, it is amazing how much we enjoy what we do.

— Transformed From Sinners to Saints —

Now that we understand names aren't just a matter of semantics, let's take a closer look at how names affect us. Before we received Christ we were called "sinners." We were professionals; our name was a job description. We were prone to sin. When we received Christ we became "saints." Paul makes this clear in his letters to the believers because he called them saints. Here are a few examples: "To all who are beloved of God in Rome, called *as* saints" (Rom. 1:7a); "To the church of God, which is at Corinth, to those who have been sanctified in Christ Jesus, *saints* by calling" (1 Cor. 1:2a); "Paul, an apostle of Christ Jesus by the will of God, to the saints who are at Ephesus and who are faithful in Christ Jesus" (Eph. 1:1). The word saint means, "holy believer." You can't be a sinner and a saint at the same time. How is it possible to be prone to sin and still be a holy believer?

The word "sinner" implies that we are prone to do wrong. If we believe we are sinners, we will sin by faith! Remember what we learned earlier, "For as [a man] thinks within himself, so he is" (Prov. 23:7). Like Jacob, trapped in deception by his name, if we still believe we are sinners, we will be unable to access the grace to live as a saint and will still try to perform good works in order to merit forgiveness. It is not our nature to sin anymore. First John 3:7-9 says,

*Little children, make sure no one deceives you; the one who practices
righteousness is righteous, just as He is righteous; the one who practices
sin is of the devil; for the devil has sinned from the beginning. The Son of
God appeared for this purpose, to destroy the works of the devil. No one
who is born of God practices sin, because His seed abides in him; and he
cannot sin, because he is born of God.*

We are Christians; it is not our nature to do wrong. Our very nature
has been changed. Now we are actually saints; righteousness is part of
our new nature and it is natural for us to glorify God. Our old man is
buried. We need to stop visiting our tombs and talking to our dead, old
man. (In the Old Testament, people were judged and killed for talking to
the dead—a practice called necromancy.) We are a new creation. It's
below our nature to act like that now—we are now princes and
princesses of the King!

The power of the cross not only dealt with the forgiveness of our
sins but it also changed our very nature. Some people have isolated the
effects of the born-again experience to the spirit. That's not accurate.
Salvation changed our entire being! Peter says that we are "partakers of
the divine nature" (2 Pet. 1:4). Think of it, your very nature is now divine!
Paul said that we are "new creatures" in Christ (2 Cor. 5:17). He didn't
say we are new spirits, he said "new creatures!" If we believe that we are
still sinners, we dilute the power of the blood and then, like Jacob,
spend our days trying to be good.

— A New Heart and a New Mind —

The truth of the matter is that we are good because we have
received a new heart and a new mind (see Ezek. 36:26; 1 Cor. 2:16).
That's right—we received a brain transplant! We actually think like God!
I have heard these verses misquoted so many times:

*"THINGS WHICH EYE HAS NOT SEEN AND EAR HAS NOT HEARD, AND
WHICH HAVE NOT ENTERED THE HEART OF MAN, ALL THAT GOD HAS PRE-
PARED FOR THOSE WHO LOVE HIM." For to us God revealed them through*

*the Spirit; for the Spirit searches all things, even the depths of God. For who among men knows the **thoughts** of a man except the spirit of the man which is in him? Even so the **thoughts** of God no one knows except the Spirit of God. Now we have received, not the spirit of the world, but the Spirit who is from God, so that we may know the things freely given to us by God, which things we also speak, not in words taught by human wisdom, but in those taught by the Spirit, combining spiritual **thoughts** with spiritual **words**. But a natural man does not accept the things of the Spirit of God, for they are foolishness to him; and he cannot understand them, because they are spiritually appraised. But he who is spiritual appraises all things, yet he himself is appraised by no one. For "WHO HAS KNOWN THE MIND OF THE LORD, THAT HE WILL INSTRUCT HIM?" But we have the mind of Christ* (1 Corinthians 2:9-16).

Did you notice that some of the text quoted above is an Old Testament verse? Paul is not saying that we don't know what God has prepared for us; he is saying that they (the Old Testament believers) didn't know what God had prepared for them because they were not "new creatures." But we have the mind of Christ because we are born of His Spirit. We think like God.

We still have a free will, and we can still choose to sin. However, as saints it doesn't come easily anymore. There is a river of God that runs through our souls and carries us towards the throne. If we don't paddle we will end up at God's house. We are prone to righteousness. That is why Paul said, "It is no longer I who live but Christ lives in me" (Gal. 2:20).

— TRYING TO DO THE RIGHT THING BUT —

Many people have misunderstood the seventh chapter of Romans. In this chapter Paul talks about his struggle with trying to do good and still doing the wrong thing. If we read these verses in light of the preceding and succeeding Scriptures, we find that it is impossible for Paul to have been speaking about his redeemed life. The entire Book of

Romans is a letter of contrast between the life lived under the Law and the life that is in Christ.

In the sixth chapter of Romans Paul teaches us that when we were baptized, we died with Christ and when we came out of the water we were raised with Him in the likeness of His resurrection. Baptism is not a symbolic act but it is a *prophetic* act. Prophetic acts, like prophetic declarations, release God's power to bring about change in our lives. In the case of baptism, being submerged under water is the act of dying with Christ, but being pulled up out of the water is equally as important as it brings power to live in Christ! This is how it reads:

> *Therefore we have been buried with Him through baptism into death, so that as Christ was raised from the dead through the glory of the Father, so we too might walk in newness of life. For if we have become united with Him in the likeness of His death, certainly we shall also be in the likeness of His resurrection, knowing this, that our old self was crucified with Him, in order that our body of sin might be done away with, so that we would no longer be slaves to sin; for he who has died is freed from sin. Now if we have died with Christ, we believe that we shall also live with Him, knowing that Christ, having been raised from the dead, is never to die again; death no longer is master over Him. For the death that He died, He died to sin once for all; but the life that He lives, He lives to God. Even so consider yourselves to be dead to sin, but alive to God in Christ Jesus* (Romans 6:4-11).

He exhorts us to therefore *consider* ourselves (that is, think about it this way) dead to sin and alive to Christ. We entered the baptismal tank with a cross and we exited with a crown! Sinning is incongruent with our new nature.

The seventh chapter begins with an analogy of a woman married to a man. Here is what Paul says:

> *Do you not know, brethren (for I am speaking to those who know the law), that the law has jurisdiction over a person as long as he lives? For the married woman is bound by law to her husband while he is living; but*

if her husband dies, she is released from the law concerning the hus-band. So then, if while her husband is living she is joined to another man, she shall be called an adulteress; but if her husband dies, she is free from the law, so that she is not an adulteress though she is joined to another man. Therefore, my brethren, you also were made to die to the Law through the body of Christ, so that you might be joined to another, to Him who was raised from the dead, in order that we might bear fruit for God (Romans 7:1-4).

Paul is giving us a description of our lives before and after Jesus. We were married to the law. The Law told us about all the things that we were doing wrong but the Law had no power to change us. When Christ died the Law was fulfilled, freeing us to marry another husband. If we have identified with Him in His death, we have entered a new covenant and are engaged to Jesus Himself. Paul goes on to make a strong connec-tion with those who struggle under the law by describing the battle he faced when he was married to the law in the present tense. But Paul declares victory in the war of his and our souls in the eighth chapter of Romans with this final blow. He says, "Therefore there is now no con-demnation for those who are in Christ Jesus. For the law of the Spirit of life in Christ Jesus has set you free from the law of sin and of death" (Rom. 8:1-2).

— Faith Is the Catalyst of the Spirit Realm —

The righteousness of God comes into our lives by faith. In order for us to believe in something we have to know that there is something to believe in. The entire spirit world operates by faith, not just God's world. For instance, fear is the manifestation that we have faith in the wrong kingdom. When we believe something is going to go wrong, we have given our faith to the enemy. By doing this we have just empowered the one that Jesus disarmed at the Cross. When we believe in God, we empower the Holy Spirit and the angels to bring about His will.

If we've been taught that after receiving Christ we are still sinners, we will struggle with trying to do the right thing because we have put our faith in our ability to fail instead of His work on the Cross! We can spend the rest of our lives living under the curse of our old name, "sinner," or like Israel, we can receive our new name that has the power to alter our very DNA. We are Saints, holy believers, and Christians, which means we are "little Christs"! When the Father looks at us, He sees the image of the Son He loves.

Chapter 6

TRAINING FOR REIGNING

*When your memories are greater than your dreams,
you are already beginning to die.*

— RAISED AS ROYALTY —

SOON after I began learning about my identity as a prince, the Lord showed me that He was commissioning me to use what I was learning to raise up an entire generation of princes and princesses. I have spent the last few years discovering the kinds of core values that develop individuals in their royal identities and promote a culture of royalty. I'll explore some of those values in the coming chapters, but in this chapter I want to look at the significance of having people who speak into our lives and call out our destinies. I've already described the negative influence many of us had in our lives from parents and others who were destructive role models. Love is always more powerful than hate. The most powerful influence we can ever have comes from positive models who have encouraged us and shown us the right way to live.

One night, still toward the beginning of my journey into the palace, the Lord began to show me Scriptures in the Book of Proverbs, which was written by Solomon—the wisest man in the Old Testament. He was the second child born to David and Bathsheba. When Bathsheba's first child died, David received a word from the Lord that Solomon would be king in David's place at the proper time. Because of this, Solomon was one of the rare leaders in the Bible who was raised to be a king from birth (see 1 Chron. 22:9-10). Written later in his life, the Book of Proverbs records the influence of his parents' teachings. David had many sons, yet

Solomon said in the Book of Proverbs, "I was a son to my father, tender and the only son in the sight of my mother, then he taught me and said to me, 'Let your heart hold fast my words'" (Prov. 4:3). He stood out from the rest of his brothers and was given special treatment and love.

Within the wisdom of the Book of Proverbs are Solomon's keys to living as royalty. For example, Proverbs 23:1-3 says: "When you sit down to dine with a ruler, consider carefully what is before you, and put a knife to your throat if you are a man of great appetite. Do not desire his delicacies, for it is deceptive food."

Notice he didn't say, "*If* you dine with a ruler," but instead, "*When* you dine with a ruler." Not IF kings invite you, but WHEN kings invite you. There was never a question that Solomon would be influential and interact with other leaders and powerful people. He could not imagine a reality where he wasn't valued and looked to, and thus had no concept of life as a pauper. Although he may have had difficulties we will not face in this day and age, he was treasured by important people around him and, most likely, never struggled with feelings of rejection, neglect or abuse. As a result of his upbringing, the Book of Proverbs is filled with sayings that reflect God's royal wisdom. Solomon lived his life according to principles of wisdom found in Proverbs, and the fame of his kingdom is attributed to these principles.

Imagine if you had been raised in a palace where every person around you told you from birth that you were destined to be a king or queen. Who would you be today and how would your life be different now? Maybe it would be easier to envision being brought up as the future President of the United States. Think about the ramifications of your childhood and how it could affect your destiny. Wouldn't you desire to do your best in life and live up to the standard of royal conduct given to you? If we know we are destined for greatness, why would we even consider abandoning that course or not living up to that potential?

The Lord showed me it is not too late to begin to think as Solomon did, to use God-given wisdom and believe in the greatness inside of us. Even if the main people who influenced us were negative role models, as Christians we now follow Christ as our example and hear the Holy

Spirit calling us into our true identities. When we begin to *act* like royalty, issues that felt like mountains in our lives will become mere stepping stones to demonstrate our character.

— LAYING OUR LIVES DOWN FOR OTHERS —

Esther, a woman we generally remember as a queen of a pagan empire in the Old Testament, was not born into a privileged life. Her life was different because she had someone who called her into her royal destiny. Mordecai, her uncle, adopted her after the death of her parents, and it is evident in Scripture that he loved her and raised her to believe she was beautiful and significant. His influence caused her to stand out.

She was selected as a candidate for queen along with many other virgins, and made an impression on the leaders of the king's guards. The Bible says, "Esther won the favor of everyone who saw her" (Esther 2:15). Even though Esther wasn't yet ready to meet the king, Mordecai's influence prepared her to excel during her year of preparation in the king's harem. There she learned the ways of royalty.

Her time of preparation was divided into two six-month sessions: the first to purify her with oil and myrrh, the second to enhance her beauty with perfumes and cosmetics. Her uncle's training and the year of intense preparation led to her triumph. The Bible records it this way, "Now the king was attracted to Esther more than to any of the other women, and she won his favor and approval more than any of the other virgins. So he set a royal crown on her head and made her queen instead of Vashti" (Esther 2:15-17). Later on in this book we will talk about the importance of Esther's rise to royalty and the way she stood up in troubled times to save the day.

— RAISED AS A PRINCESS —

Bonnie, a lady who graduated from our Supernatural School of Ministry, is a modern-day example of a woman of royalty. A year after she graduated, she became a leader in the school. When I first met Bonnie,

I realized that there was something special about her. I was interviewing her as a potential ministry school student. Over the years, I have interviewed hundreds of people for jobs and schools, but she was different. She came into my office dressed nicely and had her pen and paper ready to ask me questions about the school.

She said she was considering coming to the School of Ministry and she and her husband wanted to know what my credentials were since I was the school overseer. She wasn't like everyone else who came in trying to be impressive or begging to be accepted. She had a completely different mentality. Bonnie and her husband were trying to decide *if* we were going to *get her*. I thought I was interviewing her, but as it turns out she was interviewing me! She wanted to know where I went to school and where I received my theological degree. She asked me who I was licensed through and where I received ministerial training.

Finally, feeling a little intimidated, I admitted, "I don't have any official training, I have never been to college and I have no degree." Then I told her about an encounter I had with God and how He had called me to raise an army of warriors that would restore the ruined cities (see Isa. 61:4).

She put her pen down and stared at me, as if looking into my soul. "This is God, and I want to be a part of it," she stated.

A couple of years later she graduated from the school and we asked her to be a part of our staff. One day I was sharing my new "pauper to prince" revelation with my school staff. Bonnie was sitting with us and listened as I was discussing my ideas with the team. I was passionately exhorting the staff that we needed to understand that we are royalty; we are not paupers but princes. After about an hour of my preaching Bonnie seemed troubled and wasn't connecting with the idea.

Finally she spoke up and said, "I don't agree with what you are saying. I don't believe the issue is discovering that *we* are princes and princesses, but rather, making sure other people realize who *they* are."

I said to her, "You know why you think that is the issue? You were raised to be a princess. So the lesson for you is how to make sure people who come into your presence feel valued. I was raised as a pauper, and therefore I have to learn that I am significant first. I can't help other people feel valued until I know I am."

Bonnie had been raised as a princess and obviously is still treated as one by those who are around her. She carries herself as royalty and other people can see it. She doesn't have a problem knowing who she is, so she focuses on making sure other people catch the revelation of who they are. This is the true mentality of a prince and princess. They spend more time raising up people around them rather than worrying about their own significance. They already know who they are inside, which enables them to become selfless and give out more than they receive.

— CALLING OUT GREATNESS IN OTHERS —

We have been commissioned to develop a culture that raises up people like Solomon, Esther and Bonnie, by calling people into their royal destinies. The Bible says, "A plan in the heart of a man is like deep water, but a man of understanding draws it out" (Prov. 20:5). We need to cultivate an environment that draws out the plans God has hidden in the hearts of people. Solomon was taught to, "Train up a child in the way he should go, even when he is old he will not depart from it" (Prov. 22:6). It is important that we understand the "way people should go" so we can help them become what God has called them to be.

Prophetic ministry can play a huge part in developing a royal culture. When prophetic words are given, they are a revelation of people's true identities. This information helps leaders to know them after the Spirit, and therefore help them develop into the people they were created to be. Allison, a School of Ministry student, said to me the other day, "I love listening to other people's prophecies."

"You do?" I responded. "Why?"

"Because then I learn to treat them not as they are but as God created them to be," she answered.

Our nursery pastor, Carla, has developed a prophetic culture among the youngest of our flock. Over the nursery door a sign proclaims: "Training For Reigning." She keeps a file on every child in the nursery. She has trained her staff to prophesy over each child as they love on them, and then record the prophecies and put them into their file. As a child grows up and graduates each year from class to class, the child's file follows them so that our teachers understand the unique plan God has for each child individually. Our elementary school receives their files and continues their development with the help of this prophetic insight.

Saul's story in the Book of First Samuel further illustrates the role of prophetic ministry in revealing a person's royal destiny. His father had lost his donkeys, so he sent Saul and his servant out to find them. When they had looked for days and could not find them they decided to go to a prophet in a nearby city and see if he could tell them where the donkeys were.

Here's the biblical account:

> Now a day before Saul's coming, the Lord had revealed this to Samuel (that Saul was coming to ask for help finding his donkeys) saying, "About this time tomorrow I will send you a man from the land of Benjamin, and you shall anoint him to be prince over My people Israel; and he will deliver My people from the hand of the Philistines. For I have regarded My people, because their cry has come to Me."
>
> When Samuel saw Saul, the Lord said to him, "Behold, the man of whom I spoke to you! This one shall rule over My people."
>
> Then Saul approached Samuel in the gate and said, "Please tell me where the seer's house is."
>
> Samuel answered Saul and said, "I am the seer. Go up before me to the high place, for you shall eat with me today; and in the morning I will let you go, and will tell **you all that is on your mind**. As for your donkeys which were lost three days ago, do not set your mind on them, for they have been found. And for whom is all that is desirable in Israel? Is it not for you and for all your father's household?"

> *Saul replied, "Am I not a Benjamite, of the smallest of the tribes of Israel, and my family the least of all the families of the tribe of Benjamin? Why then do you speak to me in this way?"* (1 Samuel 9:15-21)

The most significant thing about this passage is that when Samuel tells Saul he is going to reveal to him all that has been in his mind (literally, his heart), Saul doesn't have a clue what he is talking about. He did not understand that Samuel was told to call out Saul's greatness, the greatness that was *already inside of him*.

Look what happens next:

> *Then Samuel took the flask of oil, poured it on his head, kissed him and said, "Has not the Lord anointed you a ruler over His inheritance? When you go from me today, then you will find two men close to Rachel's tomb in the territory of Benjamin at Zelzah; and they will say to you, 'The donkeys which you went to look for have been found. Now behold, your father has ceased to be concerned about the donkeys and is anxious for you, saying, "What shall I do about my son?"' Then you will go on further from there, and you will come as far as the oak of Tabor, and there three men going up to God at Bethel will meet you, one carrying three young goats, another carrying three loaves of bread, and another carrying a jug of wine; and they will greet you and give you two loaves of bread, which you will accept from their hand. Afterward you will come to the hill of God where the Philistine garrison is; and it shall be as soon as you have come there to the city, that you will meet a group of prophets coming down from the high place with harp, tambourine, flute, and a lyre before them, and they will be prophesying. Then the Spirit of the Lord will come upon you mightily, and you shall prophesy with them and be changed into another man"* (1 Samuel 10:1-6).

Samuel anoints Saul as king of Israel! Wow! Saul's call had been hidden under low self-esteem and a wrong perception of the circumstances in his life. His response to Samuel shows that he had not been raised as royalty, nor taught his true worth: "Am I not a Benjamite, of the smallest of the tribes of Israel, and my family the least of all the families of the tribe of Benjamin?" Notice how the prophetic culture that Saul encountered changed him into another man. He wasn't changed into a *different* man, but transformed *back into* the man he was created to be in the first place. The real Saul got lost in the mire of low self-esteem, sin and insignificance. Just like Saul, we all have gifts, talents and abilities; yet some of us don't believe in our potential until someone else comes alongside us and says, "Look at how much is inside of you."

Many of us have lost our true selves in the garbage of our lives. We, the church, are commissioned to develop a princely, prophetic culture that causes people's destinies to be revealed. People will then be changed back into the people they were designed to be when God conceived them.

Paul Manwaring is a pastor from England who joined our staff a few years ago. He has given our church body a realistic example of how to encourage an atmosphere of greatness. He was Governor of a prison for many years in England, and as such he was invited to the royal palace several times. He often relates these experiences with our team. He talks about how the palace itself draws out greatness in its royal subjects. Along the walls of the castle are portraits of noble people who have gone before the royal family; generations of royalty who have shaped history. Each portrait sets a standard to attain, a goal to reach and an inheritance to receive. As the royal palace sets a standard for nobility, so must we for those who are in relationship with us. We are called to be Samuels to the Sauls of our generation. Sometimes, all it takes are life-changing, prophetic words to grant us the grace to come into all that God has for us.

— CALLING OUT THE GREATNESS IN OUR FAMILIES —

In some ways, developing a royal culture in the church depends on that culture first being instilled in our families. God desires our homes to be like palaces where our children are called, trained and equipped to walk in their prophetic destinies. I don't mean that our houses have to be expensive, beautiful, or even ours, but they need to be places that remind us of our prophetic destiny and cultivate that destiny in and through us.

Our identity comes to us from the Lord but it is communicated to us first by our parents. If we have generations of healthy family life, we are more likely to know who we are. Even though Kathy and I didn't have a complete revelation of who we were when we began to raise our children, we knew that our home had to be different from our own experiences as children. Kathy and I raised our four children to be princes and princesses. They were told through our actions, words, and our love, that we valued them and they were important to us. We didn't want our children to live through the same hardships we had.

We raised our family to be empowered rather than controlled. We taught them that their opinions were valuable. We accomplished this by listening to them. When we made significant decisions, we allowed our children to be involved in our discussions because we wanted to teach them how to think, pray, and make decisions for themselves. They were permitted to question our decisions, especially the ones that affected them, providing they had the right attitude. Sometimes they even presented facts we had not been aware of, bringing new insight into situations. We were not in "no" mode while they spoke to us, and we were always willing to listen.

One of my favorite memories of empowering our children was when Jaime was 14 and Shannon was 12. They had been invited to go to China to smuggle Bibles into the country. Kathy and I immediately said, "No way! You girls are too young and China is no place for kids." Over the next couple of weeks the girls laid out their case. They reminded us that we had taught them that God protects us, that we should trust Him with our lives, and that we could even honor Him with our death. They repeated things we had been teaching them for years: "Dad, you told us we were born to change the world, to make a difference. This is a chance for God to use us and prove His faithfulness." We knew they were right, but it was difficult to practice what we had been preaching. We earnestly prayed, and then finally let them go.

They were gone for three weeks. The first thing that happened was that Jaime and another girl got caught smuggling Bibles across the border. When they were taken into the interrogation room, a Chinese woman known by reputation as the "Dragon Lady" searched them. When "Dragon Lady" stuck her hand up Jaime's dress, the other girl slapped her and they got into a fight. We were not home when one of their team called and left a message saying the girls had been arrested but that they were fine. No other information was given and we didn't hear back until a few days later. It was the longest few days of our lives. It turned out that after several hours of interrogation, the Chinese government took the Bibles away from them and miraculously let them into their country.

A week later, Shannon called from a phone booth in China. She was separated from the team and was lost in China. She didn't speak any Chinese so she couldn't figure out how to get back to her hotel. She was crying and I was trying to comfort her while I fought off my own panic. We prayed over the phone for God's help. Just as we finished our prayer, a Chinese police officer came to the phone booth and, in perfect English, asked if he could help her! He took her back to the hotel and all was well.

When the girls finally arrived in Hong Kong on their way home, they called again. They were both crying. We thought they were homesick, but actually they just didn't want to leave China. They had fallen in love with the Chinese people, and they wanted to give their lives for them. I must admit, this time I didn't listen to their argument and they safely returned home. They were changed forever by this experience, and so were we. They continued to go all over the world as teenagers. In fact, they both met their husbands on the mission field, and now co-pastor with them in two different churches on the coast of California.

Giving our families our time is also an important factor in parenting. What our children were involved in was important to us. We demonstrated this in a variety of ways, from simply being present at events to validating their worth if they ever felt rejected by peers. We went to their sports events and supported their extracurricular activities. They were involved in so many things (at one point, we had four kids in high school at the same time) that Kathy and I would often trade off going to games, and then sometimes switch at half-time. Often, we would be out four nights a week just going to their activities! Shannon and Jaime were cheerleaders and played softball, and volleyball. Eddie played basketball, baseball, soccer, and football. Jason played basketball on two teams at the same time, soccer, football, and baseball. Wow! We survived and enjoyed every minute of the chaos.

Just like Moses, our kids had no concept of what it was like to not be accepted by others. In contrast, when I was in high school, I spent my time sitting at home hoping someone would call me. I was very social, but I was raised feeling insignificant, so I thought if I called someone, they would probably not want to talk with me. My son Jason was also very social. Sometimes at night he would call eight to ten people. He had a healthy self-esteem and self-confidence. He took initiative, made a place for himself in others' lives, and assumed they would want to hear from him! It never occurred to him that someone would not want to talk with him; he had no fear of rejection.

Each child had different needs, and in one case I had to intervene to keep rejection from wounding the heart of my daughter Jaime. Jamie and Shannon arc both beautiful, but have opposite personalities. While Shannon was out socializing, being funny and making friends, Jaime would be reading, weight lifting, or other activities that were more individualized.

In high school, their youth group would have special dinners and date nights so they could have a fun and safe environment in which to learn how to cultivate a relationship with the opposite sex. Sometimes Shannon would receive five different offcrs from young men who wanted to take her out. Jaime would not be asked out at all. It seemed as if the young men were intimidated by her strong, quiet nature. The doorbell would ring, and once again Shannon would be off on another date. Jaime would climb the stairs to her room, tears running down her cheeks, and lay on her bed crying. I would find her up there, with her face in her pillow. "Daddy, why don't I ever get asked out? Is there something wrong with me? Am I ugly?" she would ask.

Inside, my heart would break for her. I would respond, "They just don't know how to take out a princess yet. Get dressed up because I'm taking you on a date." I would take her to the best places in town and we would have fun together. I think I actually took her out more often than Kathy! I wanted her to know what it was like to be taken out and have fun while being treated respectfully. Through these special times we had together, Jaime's self-confidence was protected and affirmed in a very difficult season of her life. Today, she is a confident and happy woman, wife, minister, and mother who doesn't deal with the insecurity that could have developed in high school.

— Our Commission —

As the Royal Priesthood of God, we are called to develop a culture in our homes, churches, businesses and ultimately in nations that brings out the best in individuals, facilitating their princely destinies. We do this by seeing and treating others and ourselves not as we are, but as God created us to be. This knowledge and love can only come out of intimacy with God. No longer are we His slaves, but His friends, walking by His side as kings and queens of His court.

My own struggle with insecurity is proof of the negative effect people have on our lives when they demean our value rather than affirm it. But the strength, courage, and self-esteem I see in my children, and in the examples of Solomon and Esther, are a testimony to the powerful difference it makes in people's lives when they have someone calling out their hidden greatness.

May God grant to us the insight to see beyond the outward struggles of people's lives and speak to the treasure that lies within them. May He give us wisdom to develop kings and priests, and may He endow us with the power to destroy the works of the devil!

Chapter 7

GUESS WHO IS COMING TO DINNER?

God wants to so renew our minds that He can do our will.

— SLAVES VERSUS FRIENDS —

I hope you are finally starting to comprehend that you were born into the royal family. As the King's sons and daughters, we are one of the reasons why Jesus is called "King of kings and Lord of lords" (Rev. 19:16). Jesus is not only King over the worldly kings of the earth, but He is also King over the kings that co-reign with Him in the Kingdom of God. The Book of Revelation speaks of us this way: "There will no longer be any night; and they will not have need of the light of a lamp nor the light of the sun, because the Lord God will illumine them; and they will reign forever and ever" (Rev. 22:5).

It is important we don't lose sight of the fact that God loves obedience more than sacrifice. He has never given us permission to dethrone, disrespect, or devalue Him. What many of us have not understood is that the greatness of God is actually magnified as each of His sons and daughters receive the revelation of their nobility and begin to operate in His authority. Those of us who have children understand that when our children excel and become successful, their achievements bring honor to the entire family.

Becoming friends with the God of the galaxies will dramatically increase our sense of self-worth. Jesus said:

> *You are My friends if you do what I command you. No longer do I call you slaves, for the slave does not know what his master is doing; but I*

have called you friends, for all things that I have heard from My Father I
have made known to you (John 15:14-15).

Notice the contrast between "master and slave" and "Father and friend." Jesus strikes a great balance here when He reminds us that although slaves obey out of fear, friends obey the Father out of love. A willing heart is a prerequisite to moving out of slavery into friendship. He also highlights the fact that slaves do not know what their master is doing but friends know all about the Father's business. Jesus set the example for us by doing what He saw the Father doing. If we are to do the same, we must realize that we have been invited to have the same kind of friendship with the Father that Jesus Himself had.

— THOSE WHO WALKED WITH GOD —

God had extraordinary relationships with several people through-out the Bible. The Book of Exodus says, "The Lord used to speak to Moses face to face, just as a man also to his friend" (Exod. 33:11). James says that Abraham was a friend of God (see James 2:23). Friends influence friends. These two men are an example of people who experienced a special bond with God in which the Lord invited them to influence Him.

Genesis gives insight into Abraham's relationship with God. The Lord said to Abraham, "Shall I hide from Abraham what I am about to do, since Abraham will surely become a great and mighty nation, and in him all the nations of the earth will be blessed?" (Gen. 18:17-18). God was saying to Abraham that because of the importance of his place on the earth, he was privy to inside information. Then the Lord tells Abraham that He's about to destroy Sodom. Abraham's response is surprising. He feels the freedom to interact with God, knowing that the Lord values his opinion. Look at Abraham's protest:

> *Will You indeed sweep away the righteous with the wicked? Suppose*
> *there are fifty righteous within the city; will You indeed sweep it away*
> *and not spare the place for the sake of the fifty righteous who are in it?*

Far be it from You to do such a thing, to slay the righteous with the wicked, so that the righteous and the wicked are treated alike. Far be it from You! Shall not the Judge of all the earth deal justly? (Genesis 18:23-25)

The questions he asked are important but of greater significance is the fact that he *questioned*. Where did Abraham get the idea that a human being had any right to question his Creator? What would possess a man to think that he might have a different view of a situation that God hadn't thought of? Who could ever say to God, "There are some holes in your thinking there, Lord!" However, it is in the Scriptures. A man debates with his God on the basis of his friendship.

We find the same relationship operating between God and Moses. Look at the conversation recorded in the Book of Exodus. It reads,

Then the Lord spoke to Moses, "Go down at once, for your people, whom you brought up from the land of Egypt, have corrupted themselves. They have quickly turned aside from the way, which I commanded them. They have made for themselves a molten calf, and have worshiped it and have sacrificed to it and said, 'This is your god, O Israel, who brought you up from the land of Egypt!'"

The Lord said to Moses, "I have seen this people, and behold, they are an obstinate people. Now then let Me alone, that My anger may burn against them and that I may destroy them; and I will make of you a great nation" (Exodus 32:7-10).

Moses' response floors me! Moses said to God,

Lord, why does Your anger burn against Your people whom You have brought out from the land of Egypt with great power and with a mighty hand?

Why should the Egyptians speak, saying, "With evil intent He brought them out to kill them in the mountains and to destroy them from the face of the earth?"

Turn from Your burning anger and change Your mind about doing harm to Your people. Remember Abraham, Isaac, and Israel, Your servants to whom You swore by Yourself, and said to them, "I will multiply your descendants as the stars of the heavens, and all this land of which I have spoken I will give to your descendants, and they shall inherit it forever" (Exodus 32:11-13).

Then here comes the verse that will blow our minds, ruin our theology, and bring us to the brink of an omniscient nightmare: "So the Lord changed His mind about the harm which He said He would do to His people" (Exodus 32:14).

This amazing story highlights an intimate relationship between a man and his God. Here an unredeemed human, living under the old covenant, finds a place with the God of all creation, the wisest Being in the entire universe, and tells Him that destroying His own people is simply a bad idea. Their conversation reveals a deep sense of mutual respect.

God, angry at Israel, tries to put the responsibility for the people on Moses by telling Moses, "These are your people whom you brought out of Egypt." "On the contrary," Moses says to God, "These are *Your* people whom *You* brought out of Egypt."

This conversation reminds me of times when I used to come home from work and my wife, Kathy, would try to disown one of our children because they had made trouble during the day. She would say, "Your son Jason wrote on the walls with color crayons today." He was always *my* son when he was misbehaving and *her* son when he was acting like an angel.

Underneath the dialogue between God and Moses lies a deeper question. Was God saying to Moses, "Boy, Moses, I never thought about those Israelites being My people or about My reputation with those Egyptians. I am sure glad I have you around so I don't forget these things"? I don't think so! This may shock you but I don't think God always wants to be right when He speaks to us! God often restrains His strength so that He can have a relationship with His people!

— His Restraint for Our Friendship —

Recently I experienced what it must feel like for God to restrain His strength for the sake of having a relationship with His children. My grandson Elijah came over to our house. He ran into my bedroom yelling, "Papa, let's wrestle!" Then he jumped on my bed and landed on me as hard as he could, hitting and kicking me with everything he had.

I didn't grab him and throw him through the window yelling, "Take that, Spiderman!" Instead, I restrained my strength so that we could have fun. I spent most of the time trying to make sure that he didn't fall off the bed and hurt himself. In the same way, God, who is beyond our understanding, welcomes us to interact with Him by "tying most of His brain behind His back" and leaving room for His friends' advice.

Unfortunately, the church has had a single-dimensional view of what it means to have a relationship with God. We have overemphasized obedience and underemphasized friendship. This has resulted in our interactions with the Almighty becoming robotic and soldier-like. Men and women of old understood something that, centuries later, we are still trying to figure out: *God wants friends, not slaves!*

What is the secret to the relationship that Abraham and Moses had with God? How did they get welcomed into His Majesty's Secret Service? The next chapter of Exodus offers more insight on these questions. It reads:

> *Then the Lord said to Moses, "Depart, go up from here, you and the people whom you have brought up from the land of Egypt, to the land of which I swore to Abraham, Isaac, and Jacob, saying, 'To your descendants I will give it.' I will send an angel before you and I will drive out the Canaanite, the Amorite, the Hittite, the Perizzite, the Hivite and the Jebusite. Go up to a land flowing with milk and honey; for I will not go up in your midst, because you are an obstinate people, and I might destroy you on the way"* (Exodus 33:1-3).

But Moses said to the Lord:

> *"See, You say to me, 'Bring up this people!' But You Yourself have not let me know whom You will send with me. Moreover, You have said, 'I have known you by name, and you have also found favor in My sight.' Now therefore, I pray You, if I have found favor in Your sight, let me know Your ways that I may know You, so that I may find favor in Your sight. Consider too, that this nation is Your people."*
>
> *And He said, "My presence shall go with you, and I will give you rest."*
>
> *Then he said to Him, "If Your presence does not go with us, do not lead us up from here. For how then can it be known that I have found favor in Your sight, I and Your people? Is it not by Your going with us, so that we, I and Your people, may be distinguished from all the other people who are upon the face of the earth?"*
>
> *Then the Lord said to Moses, "I will also do this thing of which you have spoken; for you have found favor in My sight and I have known you by name"* (Exodus 33:12-17).

Look at what happened in these verses.

God said, "I will fulfill My promises to your forefathers by sending My angel to escort you, but I am not going with you." Many of us would have been happy with our prayers being answered by the Lord's sending an angel to go with us. I often wonder if we would have even recognized whether we had the angel of the Lord with us and not the Lord.

Moses proves his friendship with God when he said, "If you're not going to the Promised Land, I am not going either!" Moses was saying to God, "You are more important to me than any vision that I have for my life." This is a key to building a deeper relationship with the Father. We must want Him more than we want what He does. Wherever you find people who love Jesus more than they love the world, you will discover a place that is filled with the joy of friendship.

— TESTING OUR HEARTS —

We need to realize that sometimes when the Lord prophesies to us, He is testing our hearts more than He is determining our destiny. Paul realized this. In the Book of Acts, a prophet named Agabus came down from Judea, took Paul's belt, bound his own feet and hands, and said,

> *"This is what the Holy Spirit says: 'In this way the Jews at Jerusalem will bind the man who owns this belt and deliver him into the hands of the Gentiles.' ...Then Paul answered, 'What are you doing, weeping and breaking my heart? For I am ready not only to be bound, but even to die at Jerusalem for the name of the Lord Jesus'"* (Acts 21:11,13).

Many of us would have taken this as a directional word from the Lord to not go to Jerusalem since we might be imprisoned. It would probably never occur to us that God still wanted Paul to go on to Jerusalem and ultimately to Rome so that he could speak to Caesar. Our concept of God does not allow the Lord to speak to us without believing that He is giving us a direct command that we must obey unthinkingly. It seems like heresy for someone to even suggest that sometimes when God prophesies to us, He is looking more for interaction than He is for blind obedience.

What kind of relationship would we have with our friends if we demanded our own way any time we got together? What would it be like if you had to eat at the restaurant that I liked, go to the movies that I enjoyed and talk about the things that I wanted to talk about? With that attitude, it wouldn't be long before I'd find myself alone. The famous chapter on love in the Book of First Corinthians says that some of the attributes of love are that it *"does not seek its own"* and that it *"takes no thought for itself"* (1 Cor. 13:5). We forget sometimes that the love the Bible is talking about here describes the nature of God before it ever applies to us. God is not selfish. He isn't just hanging around with us so He can get His way. He practices what He preaches!

David is another Old Testament believer who, "being a man after God's own heart," transcended the rules of his day and established a friendship with God. In those days there were strict laws concerning how the people of God could worship. Only the high priest could go in before the ark of God one day per year. David erected a tabernacle and had the priests minister before the Ark of the Covenant 24 hours a day, seven days a week, for more than 30 years. Not only did David get away with doing something that was against the law of God, but in the Book of Acts, it says that God liked it so much that He's going to rebuild it in the last days (see Acts 15:16-18)!

David's friendship with God was so extraordinary that he wanted to build a temple for God. God told David that although He didn't live in a house that was made by the hands of men, He would allow David's son, Solomon, to build Him one anyway. Then at the temple dedication Solomon repeated God's words:

> *"Since the day that I brought My people Israel from Egypt, I did not choose a city out of all the tribes of Israel in which to build a house that My name might be there, but I chose David to be over My people Israel." Now it was in the heart of my father David to build a house for the name of the Lord, the God of Israel* (1 Kings 8:16-17).

Isn't this exciting? It wasn't God's idea to build a house for Himself—it was God's idea to choose David. It was in the heart of David to do something for God. We should note that David was not doing the will of the Father but he was doing his own will. The Lord loved it because it was coming from the heart of a friend. Friendship transcends obedience!

Christians have a special place in the heart of the Father. God has even given us permission to forgive the sins of other people. He made this radical statement to drive His point home, "If you forgive the sins of any, their sins have been forgiven them; if you retain the sins of any, they have been retained" (John 20:23). Consider the ramifications of withholding forgiveness from someone—yet the Lord trusts us with these important decisions.

John the apostle, who laid his head on the breast of Christ, had incredible insight into the heart of God. Here he finds the courage to record the following words that came from the mouth of Jesus himself, "If you abide in Me, and My words abide in you, ask whatever you wish, and it will be done for you" (John 15:7). Notice how being in right relationship with God gives us permission to ask for whatever we wish. The Bible is full of verses like this one. We are so accustomed to viewing the Scriptures through a slave's mentality it seldom dawns on us that God actually likes the fact that we have a will. It was His idea to give us a brain.

— TRUE INTIMACY —

There are so many Christians who, without realizing it, have not heard the higher call of intimacy in their walk with God. This truth pierced the heart of one of my friends. Kevin and I were driving down the road making small talk and I offered him a candy bar.

He said, "No thanks, seven years ago God told me to fast sugar. I haven't eaten candy since then."

I asked him why God told him not to eat sugar. It suddenly got very quiet in the car. We drove along for several minutes without talking and then I finally asked him again, thinking that he hadn't heard me. "Kevin, why did God tell you not to eat sugar?"

"I heard you! I heard you!" he said. Kevin continued, "It just occurred to me that I never asked God why. I just realized that my relationship with God has been based on obedience and not on friendship."

God wants to build trust and honor His people. This is underscored in Second Chronicles 20:20: "O Judah and inhabitants of Jerusalem, put your trust in the Lord your God and you will be established. Put your trust in His prophets and succeed." This same concept resounds in the Book of Exodus. God said to Moses, "Behold, I will come to you in a thick cloud, so that the people may hear when I speak with you and may also believe in you forever" (Exod. 19:9). God performed signs and wonders not just so the people would believe in Him, but believe in Moses also, forever!

The struggle with much of the teaching in this book is that when some people read about friendship with God, they tend to grab hold of the "-ship," the vehicle, without making friends with God. These same people love structure, formulas and principles, but without relationship (another "-ship"). Without the *heart* of friendship, they become danger-ous and destructive while the teaching gets branded as heresy. When someone who is not a friend uses the privileges of friendship, there is a violation of relationship. I encourage my friends to make themselves at home in my house. If someone I don't know walks into my house, opens my refrigerator and starts eating my food, I'm not okay with that. We call these people thieves, not friends.

We have been invited to the marriage supper of the Lamb, not just as a guest, but as the Bride. This is not a shotgun wedding, nor does the Bridegroom want to marry a silly slave girl with half a brain. No! He's looking for a Proverbs 31 woman. Someone He can brag about in the gates, who is beautiful, noble, and faithful. He's looking for an intimate friend who will not simply partner with Him, but also walk by His side, conversing and discussing His plans for the world. Just as we desire healthy and deep relationships with those around us, He wishes this with us. What a privilege!

Part II:
Introducing
the Attributes of Royalty

THIS manuscript is not intended to be the last word on kingly heritage or the final word on the behavior of princes. Instead, it is written to be a catalyst toward royal thinking.

Many exceptional books have been written about the character of Christians and the fruit of the Spirit. If I were attempting to paint a complete picture of God's amazing people, I would have to include information from many of those books. As a matter of fact, several of the greatest virtues of royalty such as love, loyalty, honesty, purity, diligence, joy, faithfulness, responsibility, patience, wisdom, generosity, and integrity (the list goes on and on), have not been included here.

Instead, I've emphasized qualities that are at the core of biblical thinking, yet are nearly forgotten. Let's journey into the palace for a closer look at the heart of the King of all kings and the way of His royal people.

Chapter 8

SUPERHEROES IN THE SANCTUARY

Children never fight over who is going to be the garbage man. We learn that in church and it is killing us!

— THE BATTLE OF THE SUPERHEROES —

Ientered the family room just as a fierce argument broke out between three of my grandchildren, who were wrestling on the floor.

Five-year-old Elijah yelled, "I'm Spiderman," and shot an imaginary web at Isaac, who was four.

Isaac protested, "I'm Spiderman!"

"No, you can't be Spiderman," Elijah insisted, establishing his rank with his younger cousin. "I am already Spiderman! You can be Superman."

Just then Rilie, Elijah's three-year-old sister, shouted, "I wanna be Spiderman! I wanna be Spiderman!"

In a stern voice Elijah said, "Rilie, you have to be someone else! You can't be Spiderman! I am already Spiderman!"

"Papa!" she cried. "Elijah isn't sharing. He is not playing fair! He won't let me be Spiderman!"

"Rilie," I said, taking her in my arms, "why don't you be Wonder Woman? Wonder Woman can whip Spiderman and she is beautiful like you."

"Okay," she responded, as I wiped away her tears.

One of the things I have observed by watching my seven grandchildren play is that they never fight over who's going to be the garbage man. They have argued over who will be the beautiful princess, Batman, Spiderman, Superman, or other super heroes, some of whom I have never heard of before. Yet, they never squabble over being a "loser."

Each of us, in our own areas of life, has desired greatness and want to be known as a hero. We are no different than Jesus' disciples. Every time He stepped away from them, they would fight over which one of them was the greatest. These contests escalated to the point that James and John talked their mother into asking Jesus if her sons could sit on His left and right in Heaven! I have often imagined what their fights must have looked like.

Matthew: "Did you see that blind man I healed yesterday? He had been blind since birth."

Peter: "That was nothing. I ministered to a guy who was blind and lame from a donkey accident he had when he was a little boy!"

Judas: "Oh yeah? Well have you guys ever taken an offering like this?" (pulling a pouch of coins out of his pocket).

Thomas: "I really doubt it."

James and John—who are called the Sons of Thunder—say in unison:

"That makes me mad!"

It seems like Jesus spent a lot of time trying to get the boys to stop competing with each other. He put a kid in the middle of the group and gave them an object lesson on entering the Kingdom as a child. He stripped down, washed their feet, and taught them about humility. He clarified that everyone was important in His Kingdom, no matter how insignificant a person may seem. Paul echoes Jesus when he says,

> *For I say, through the grace given to me, to everyone who is among you, not to think of himself more highly than he ought to think, but to think soberly, as God has dealt to each one a measure of faith. For as we have many members in one body, but all the members do not have the same function, so we, being many, are one body in Christ, and individually members of one another* (Romans 12:3-5 NKJV).

He told them stories about being invited to a party and choosing a seat that did not reflect their importance. But nothing He did seemed to take away their *desire for greatness*. Greatness has been bred into us from birth. Someone had to teach us to *want* to be losers. When we were children we wanted to be someone special; unfortunately the church has a way of beating that out of us by legalism and performance. We can do nothing to earn our Father's love. By simply "being" ourselves, we are precious and already glorious in His sight.

We need to get back to childlikeness in order to understand how exceptional we are to Him. Children who are being brought up in a healthy home know that their parents adore them and would do anything to protect them. They can do nothing to earn their parent's love because their parents loved them before they were conceived, just as our Father loved us before we could even know how to love Him: "We love Him because He first loved us" (1 John 4:19 NKJV). We were wonderfully made from the beginning; it is part of our divine nature!

— GOD LIVES OUTSIDE OF TIME —

We were created for glory from the beginning of time. Let's look at how God's timeless zone affects the glorious call of God on our lives. According to earth's perspective, Jesus was crucified almost 2,000 years ago. However, the Bible says that Jesus was slain from the foundation of the world: "All who dwell on the earth will worship him, whose names have not been written in the Book of Life of the Lamb slain from the foundation of the world" (Rev. 13:8 NKJV).

God lives outside of time. When God said, "Let there be light," He not only created night and day, He created *time*. The spirit world lives in the timeless zone. Picture time like a train moving through the Lord's Kingdom. The engine represents the beginning of time and the caboose symbolizes the end of time. God is able to get on anywhere on that train. He knows what's going to happen in the future because *He has already been there*. God is not bound by time. Peter knew this truth when he said, "Do not let this one fact escape your notice, beloved, that with the Lord one day is like a thousand years, and a thousand years like one day" (2 Pet. 3:8).

When Jesus died on the cross He descended into Sheol and rescued all those who were imprisoned by the devil (Eph 4:8-10). He was gone from earth for three days, yet He passed from a time zone into a *timeless* zone. We understand from the story of Lazarus in Luke 16 that Sheol was the holding place for all those who died *before* Jesus paid the price for their sins with His blood. It had two areas with a chasm separating each. On one side was Hades, which was for people who were waiting to go into hell. On the other side was Abraham's bosom, which was the holding place for the righteous. Because Sheol was an eternal place, existing outside of time, we were also captive there!

When Jesus descended into Sheol, took the host of captives and ascended to Heaven, we were with Him! Paul describes this in the Book of Ephesians. It states:

> *When He ascended on high, He led captive a host of captives and He gave gifts to men. Now this expression, "He ascended," what does it mean except that He also had descended into the lower parts of the earth? He who descended is Himself also He who ascended far above all the heavens, so that He might fill all things* (Ephesians 4:8-10).

Paul goes on to say that we are seated with Christ in heavenly places—meaning, *now*! Though we are right here on earth, God is speaking to us from the *timeless* zone. He always speaks to us as if it has already happened because in *His* world it has!

Long ago, the Lord spoke to Jeremiah from eternity and said, "Before I formed you in the womb I knew you, and before you were born I consecrated you; I have appointed you a prophet to the nations" (Jer. 1:5). People teach all kinds of strange doctrine from this verse, but it simply confirms that He does not live in the same time zone that we do.

It might help us to understand how God relates to time if we think about the way we view the stars. Light travels at 186,000 miles per second. The stars are thousands of light-years away. Therefore, some of the bright stars that we see in the sky burned out long ago. The light we perceive now is an old message from a dead star. In other words, we are viewing something today that actually happened thousands of years ago. It's as if we are going back into time when we view the stars!

Why is time so important? By understanding how God is outside of time, we will understand how He chose us long ago to make us glorious like Him!

— PREDESTINED FOR GLORY —

Romans 8:28 is popular to quote when we are in trouble or having a bad day. It says, "We know that God causes all things to work together for good to those who love God, to those who are called according to His purpose." What most of us have not understood is *why* all things work together for good. Look at the next two verses:

> *For those whom He foreknew, He also predestined to become conformed to the image of His Son, so that He would be the firstborn among many brethren; and these whom He predestined, He also called; and these whom He called, He also justified; and these whom He justified, He also glorified* (Romans 8:29-30).

Those He "foreknew" He also predestined for glory. God has already gone into our future and worked out all the circumstances so that we can become more glorious! That's why all things work together for good, because God created us with the end in mind. God starts from the end and works backward. He has looked at the finished product of His finest creation and said, "You are awesome!" Romans 9:22-24 (NKJV) says it like this:

> *What if God, wanting to show His wrath and to make His power known, endured with much longsuffering the vessels of wrath prepared for destruction, and that He might make known the riches of His glory on the vessels of mercy, which He had prepared beforehand for glory, even us whom He called, not of the Jews only, but also of the Gentiles?*

He prepared us beforehand for glory. God hid wisdom for OUR glory. First Corinthians 2:7 says, "We speak God's wisdom in a mystery, the hidden wisdom which God predestined before the ages to our glory." Paul said that we are being transformed by going from glory to a greater glory: "But we all, with unveiled face, beholding as in a mirror the glory of the Lord, are being transformed into the same image from glory to glory, just as from the Lord, the Spirit" (2 Cor. 3:18).

Ephesians 1:4 says, "He chose us in Him before the foundation of the world, that we should be holy and without blame before Him in love." That is why Romans says, "Whom He foreknew." God knew what we would be and do before we were ever conceived. He didn't make our choices for us, but He knew what they would be because in *His* world they have already happened. He knew that we would choose Him, so He chose us first. It is powerful to think that He knows us so well that He knew to choose us before we even knew whether or not we would choose Him!

The writer of Hebrews says that Jesus died to bring many sons to glory! "For it was fitting for Him, for whom are all things, and through whom are all things, in bringing many sons to glory, to perfect the author of their salvation through sufferings" (Heb. 2:10). We know that we have an incredible inheritance in God, but do we realize that we are His glorious inheritance? Paul states in Ephesians, "I pray that the eyes of your heart may be enlightened, so that you will know what is the hope of His calling, what are the riches of the glory of His inheritance in the saints" (Eph. 1:18).

In essence, we must realize that the promises in these Scripture are *for us*. He loves us so much that we are to become His glorious inheritance! We were created for glory. Before the foundations of the earth, we were made and predestined for greatness because He already knew we would choose Him. He set up our lives in such a way that we could not help but be awesome. You now have a right to believe you are indescribably irresistible just the way you were made! By choosing us first, He gave us the inheritance of greatness, for we are commissioned to be like Him, and He is glorious! What a remarkable thought! Praise God that His love is simple—He just LOVES US, no more and no less.

Chapter 9

ALL THE WAY DOWN TO THE TOP

The truth of God's grace humbles a man without degrading him and exalts a man without inflating him.

— WHO IS YOUR DADDY? —

RECENTLY I was leading a prophetic training session at a ministry school. We began the class by talking about the primary purpose of prophetic ministry and started to share that our first priority as a prophetic person is to find the treasure God has hidden in the life of each and every person He has created. In the middle of telling them that we are to "discover and call out the greatness that the Lord had hidden in the lives of people," one of the pastors joined us from another room. I had never met him before and I was unaware at the time that he was part of the leadership team.

Before I could go on, he said, "I have a question for you."

"Okay," I responded, "what is it?"

"I think God is great," he said.

"Yeah, and...did I say something that made you think I don't believe that God is great?" I asked.

"You said that people are 'great.' I think you are teaching a doctrine that promotes pride in people by trying to discover the greatness that is in them," he continued.

I was becoming just a little "fried," so I responded, "I believe that religion emasculates and castrates people in the name of humility!"

We were sitting in a room that had a beautiful picture on the wall next to us. I pointed to the painting and said to him, "Let's pretend that you were the artist who painted that picture."

"Okay," he said, looking a little uptight.

I motioned to the picture and yelled, "What a stupid-looking painting! Those colors are terrible! That thing is so ugly!" I paused for a minute. "Now," I said to him, "does demeaning the painting somehow glorify the artist?"

"No!" he answered.

Now I had him cornered, so I continued, "Not only is God Himself the one who painted us, so to speak, but Jesus was the one who sat in the chair and modeled for the masterpiece! Remember, we were made in God's image and in His likeness. We didn't create ourselves. God created us. We are the work of His hands. When we tear ourselves down we aren't being humble, we are being stupid!"

He looked stunned. He said, "I have three theological degrees, yet I've never been taught this."

— PRIDE VERSUS EXALTATION OF GOD —

This encounter confirmed to me once again that there is a lie still alive and well in the minds of many Christians, a lie which strategically keeps us from walking in the fullness of our identity in Christ. This lie tells us that any recognition of our strength or goodness is pride, and that the only way to deal with pride is to demean ourselves, which is humility. The truth is that it is neither pride to recognize our strengths nor humility to demean them. This kind of false humility keeps the saints in darkness and results in us never stepping into our destinies.

Remember what we just saw in the previous chapter? Romans 3:23 says that we, "fell short of the glory of God." Though we missed it, we were made for glory. Thankfully, when Jesus died on the cross, He didn't just die so He could forgive our sins. He died so we could be restored to our original purpose. The price that Jesus paid on the Cross determined the value of the people He purchased. We were created to share God's glory and bring Him glory. After all, who is greater—a king over a bunch of bozos, or a king over a great army of confident soldiers who take pride in serving their king? Isn't it true that the greatness of the King's subjects actually glorify the King Himself?

The account of King Nebuchadnezzar's dream in the fourth chapter of Daniel shows us that learning humility doesn't mean we have to think of ourselves negatively. In the dream Nebuchadnezzar sees an angel cut down a huge tree, leaving only the stump. Daniel, his most trusted dream interpreter, tells him that the dream is about him. He is the tree, and he is about to get cut down because of his pride. Daniel urges the king to humble himself before God humbles him.

Twelve months later, Nebuchadnezzar is on the roof of his castle talking to himself about how awesome he is to have accomplished so much by himself. Suddenly he loses his mind. He is driven into the fields and lives like an animal for seven years. Finally, after seven long years of complete insanity, God restores his mind. The first statement out of his mouth when he can finally talk again is stunning:

> *At that time my reason returned to me. And my majesty and splendor were restored to me for the glory of my kingdom, and my counselors and my nobles began seeking me out; so I was reestablished in my sovereignty, and surpassing greatness was added to me* (Daniel 4:36).

If we didn't know better, wouldn't we think that this was the kind of statement that provoked God to humble him in the first place? Once again, he is saying, "I am awesome!" But look at the next verse! He says, "Now I, Nebuchadnezzar, praise, exalt and honor the King of heaven, for all His works are true and His ways just, and He is able to humble those who walk in pride" (Dan. 4:37).

Did you get that? King Nebuchadnezzar is saying that he's awesome, but God is more awesome. God's problem with Nebuchadnezzar was not his greatness, but his taking all the credit for it without acknowledging that God gave him his kingdom in the first place. God gave him back everything he had lost because he learned his lesson, that "Heaven rules" (Dan. 4:26). The point is that as long as we acknowledge where our greatness comes from, we're not in danger of pride. We don't glorify God by saying we're not great, we glorify Him by acknowledging that He is the source of that greatness. Humility is not demeaning ourselves but exalting our God.

By telling us that "humility" means convincing ourselves we are "nobodies," many Christian leaders have sold God's people into theological slavery. This belief system has not cured pride but has worked to destroy the confidence of God's people. True humility is not the absence of confidence but *strength restrained*. The only way we can truly be humble is to have an *honest assessment of ourselves before God*. If we know we deserve the highest seat in the house and we take a lower seat than we deserve, we have humbled ourselves. If we deserve a low seat and we take the low seat, it is not called humility. If we don't know what seat we belong in and we sit in a lower seat than we deserve, we got lucky because the head of the household is not going to humiliate us by asking us to move down. Humility is an issue of the heart. We can't be humble by accident; we must purpose in our heart to know our greatness yet never exalt ourselves higher than we ought. Scripture says that Moses "was very humble, more than all men who were on the face of the earth" (Num. 12:3 NKJV). Interestingly, it was Moses himself who wrote the first five books of the Bible, including this verse. He had an inspired, honest assessment of himself before God, so he didn't contradict himself by saying he was the most humble man on earth.

We can be people of humility and still be confident in who we are. Unfortunately, confidence always looks like arrogance to the insecure. Here is where the real issue lies. I believe that behind the false humility promoted by some Christian leaders is a conviction that they and everyone else are actually not worth much. In their "honest assessment of their abilities" they still see themselves as fallen people. It's another example of the pauper mentality at work. We have spiritualized our low self-esteem and that is wrong!

God has given the church a great call, and therefore it takes great people to accomplish it. If we fail to see our greatness, we will fall short of our call. Our pauper mentality and false humility have rendered much of the Church ineffective by diminishing our vision for the influence we are meant to have in the world. We can see this in the way we have perceived and pursued the Great Commission. In Matthew 28, Jesus gives us instructions on how worldwide revival is to take place: It is to begin with believers making disciples of the nations. We have reduced our Lord's Great Commission down to something we are more comfortable with, which is ministering to individuals rather than nations. We will talk more about this later. We usually target economically poor and broken individuals over individuals with influence and status. Our insecurity causes us to feel disqualified to reach the rich, educated, and powerful.

— HEROES OF THE GENERATIONS —

Scripture describes men and women of God who took hold of the positions of influence that had been offered to them and recognized that God was strategically placing them there. Their greatness was not for their own benefit, but to give the world a taste of the Kingdom of God. Today, where are the people like Joseph who will become a "father" to the Pharaohs of the world and see whole nations fall into the hands of God? (See Genesis 45.) What has happened to the Elijahs who confronted kings and changed history with their prophetic proclamations? What has become of people like Daniel, who stood in the courts of four worldly kings and won the most powerful nations of the time to God? Why aren't the Nehemiahs of our day around to rebuild our ruined cities? Why is it that giants such as abortion, homosexuality, racism, crime, and corruption are continually allowed to roam the earth and wreak havoc on our children while the people of God cower behind pews, hoping our government will pass a law to stop the big guys?

We have been called to teach the nations how to stop giants, prosper in famines, rebuild cities and restore fathers to lost children! Every time someone like David or Joseph gets confident enough to rise from obscurity and change the course of history, some church leader, like Joseph's or David's brothers, slaps a "pride" label on them and gives them a lesson in feeling bad about themselves.

The lesson usually seems to end with a class on the art of "cross-carrying." We have made cross-carrying a career opportunity instead of a one-day event. This derives from a serious misunderstanding of what happened to us when we were saved. When Jesus told us to take up our cross and follow Him, He wasn't talking about spending our whole life with a cross on our back, anymore than He did. We are meant to take up our cross and follow Jesus to the baptismal tank, where we identify with Him in His death. Paul says that:

> *We were buried with Him through baptism into death, that just as Christ was raised from the dead by the glory of the Father, even so we also should walk in the newness of life. For if we have been united together in the likeness of His death, certainly we shall also be in the likeness of His resurrection...For the death that He died, He died to sin once for all; but the life that He lives, He lives to God* (Romans 6:6-10).

We are supposed to enter the death chamber of baptism with a cross and exit with a crown. The crown is, "The likeness of His resurrection!" The apostle John said, "As He is, (speaking of Jesus) so also are we in this world" (1 John 4:17). Notice he didn't say, "As He was" but instead he said, "As He is." Jesus is not the suffering servant carrying His Cross anymore. He is the coming King. We are to be the revelation of His royalty on the earth. Paul emphasized this to the Corinthian church, "You are already filled, you have already become rich, you have become kings without us; and indeed, I wish that you had become kings so that we also might reign with you" (1 Cor. 4:8).

The full revelation of what it means to be saved still needs to penetrate our thinking until we understand that who we were is totally dead and who we are is the revelation of Christ on the earth. When we came to Christ, it *was* humility to honestly assess ourselves as sinners. To go back and say that's still who we are is to deny what Christ did for us.

Doing that is no longer humbling ourselves, it's undercutting the resurrection power God has given us to live like Him.

— FALSE HUMILITY —

Several years ago, there was a prophecy given that continues to circulate through our churches today. The prophecy was that this last day's revival will be ushered in by a "nameless and faceless generation." I understand most people think this is an accurate prophecy that communicates that God wants to use everybody and not just famous people. I do agree that God wants to work through all of us to rock the world. However, I think the church often prophesies out of a pauper mentality and operates in false humility. The point I am trying to make here is that there are no little people in the Kingdom of God. There are only sons and daughters who are more than conquerors!

Instead of saying God wants to use "little people like us" to make the point that everyone is useful to God, we should remind people (that is, RE-mind or give them a new mind) of their royal identity. After all, God spends many chapters of the Bible "boring us" with generation after generation of the names of His people who were involved in some historic event. God even acknowledges that Jesus Christ was rooted in humanity by naming Him in the entire genealogy of Joseph. (Joseph wasn't even His real father.) But this prophecy says that the revival will be "nameless and faceless." False humility steals our names and defaces our identities until we are harmless against the powers of darkness.

God never reminds us of our smallness when He calls us to do something awesome. Instead He calls us to courage by proclaiming something amazing over us like, "You're a mighty warrior," "A father of many nations," or "You're the one that all of Israel is waiting on!" Unlike God, the typical Christian culture embraces smallness to include people who feel insignificant. The consequence is that we've shrunk men below the size of their devil and so they are left to face him without the full benefit of their true identity and authority. We must be elevated to capture the high calling of God, as Paul states in Philippians 3:14 (KJV),

"I press toward the mark for the prize of the high calling of God in Christ Jesus."

It is essential that the Body of Christ gets free from an ungodly, low self-esteem. We see throughout Scripture that when people get an identity change from God, they are catapulted into the destiny that once eluded them. Gideon was a young man who was destined to change the course of history. Like most of us, his low self-esteem had promoted a false humility in him that reduced his life down to simply making a living. His story reads:

> The angel of the Lord appeared to him and said to him, "The Lord is with you, O valiant warrior." Then Gideon said to him, "O my lord, if the Lord is with us, why then has all this happened to us? And where are all His miracles which our fathers told us about, saying, 'Did not the Lord bring us up from Egypt?' But now the Lord has abandoned us and given us into the hand of Midian." The Lord looked at him and said, "Go in this your strength and deliver Israel from the hand of Midian. Have I not sent you?" He said to Him, "O Lord, how shall I deliver Israel? Behold, my family is the least in Manasseh, and I am the youngest in my father's house" (Judges 6:12-15).

The angel knows that Israel's deliverance rests on his ability to impact Gideon's self-esteem. Like Gideon, many of us are fed up with the evils that surround us, yet it hasn't occurred to us that the miracle we have been praying for already lies within us. When God called him a "valiant warrior," Gideon was able to step into an identity that allowed him to bring about the justice that his heart yearned for. It is important for us to realize here that although it appeared that the Midianites were Israel's oppressors, the real bondage lay inside of Gideon.

His response to the angel gives us insight into the actual source of Gideon's fear. He said, "Is my family not the least in Manasseh and I am not the youngest?" His problem isn't so much that the enemy is so big but that he feels so small. You can always tell the size of a man's identity by the size of the problem it takes to discourage him. It is also interesting to note that when the people of God fought the Midianites they yelled, *"A sword for the Lord and for Gideon!"* (Judg. 7:20). Because Gideon rose to become the leader God destined him to be, the people were loyal to both God and Gideon.

False humility is running rampant in the Body of Christ! We hear it after a person sings a great song in church. When we tell them what an awesome job they did, it is common for them to say something like, "It wasn't me; it was Jesus." I often want to say to them, "It wasn't that good!" This mentality is killing us because we don't want people to think there is anything good in us. This leads to the same bondage Gideon experienced. Life seems so dangerous and we feel so vulnerable.

— THE WAR AROUND US —

When we do finally win the war inside ourselves, another battlefield begins to develop around us as the enemy tries to disempower us through fear. The life of Nehemiah illustrates this beautifully. Nehemiah, unlike Gideon, knew who he was in God and understood his life call was to alter the course of history by rebuilding the walls of Jerusalem and establishing a government in Israel after their many years in exile. The Israelites had been trying to reconstruct the walls for years, yet the enemy had managed to scare them back into their "pews." Let's look at the dialog between Nehemiah and his detractors.

Ono means "strength"and it represents the place of the enemy's strength. It is important for us to not fall for the tactics of the enemy by going down to the valley of his strength. If you venture down there, you will discover why the place is called "Oh No!" Nehemiah demonstrates how to stay out of this valley of trouble. He proclaims to his adversary, "I am doing a great work and I cannot come down to you?"Wow! This isn't pride, but the confidence of a man who knows his God, knows himself, and knows his assignment.

Later on the enemy tries to get Nehemiah to hide in the church saying, "Let us meet together in the house of God, within the temple, and let us close the doors of the temple, for they are coming to kill you, and they are coming to kill you at night."

Nehemiah said,

> *"Should a man like me flee? And could one such as I go into the temple to save his life? I will not go in." Then I perceived that surely God had not sent him, but he uttered his prophecy against me because Tobiah and Sanballat had hired him. He was hired for this reason, that I might become frightened and act accordingly and sin, so that they might have an evil report in order that they could reproach me. Remember, O my God, Tobiah and Sanballat according to these works of theirs, and also Noadiah the prophetess and the rest of the prophets who were trying to frighten me* (Nehemiah 6:11-14).

When we wallow in low self-esteem and false humility we are powerless to stop the onslaughts of the devil. Satan uses the "doctrine of humility" to castrate our confidence and paralyze the people of God. This false doctrine teaches us that being confident that we our doing a "great work for God" is arrogance. This belief system is expressed in statements like "It's not me. It is just Jesus." This is not true! Jesus has commissioned us to co-labor with Him. He called us to reign with Him.

The enemy has also polluted much of the prophetic movement with his "Noadiah" prophecies that are designed to "frighten us." These "prophets" run around the world prophesying their message of doom, reducing the Body of Christ to scared children.

Satan fears that the Church will gain back her confidence and begin to restore our ruined cities. He works overtime to tell us how weak the church is, how dark the day is and how angry our Father is with us. This is all a bunch of lies!

— HUMILITY DESCRIBED —

I am not at all trying to promote pride, arrogance, or brashness. I simply want to define what true humility is. No one can stand to be around people who are stuck on themselves. It's sickening to be in the presence of a person who is self-centered or believes themselves to be self-made. When we feel bad about ourselves, we have also made ourselves the center of attention. This is every bit as arrogant as the person who walks around telling people how much better he is than everyone else. Humility isn't thinking less of ourselves but thinking of ourselves less.

True humility is born out of an awareness of God's greatness, grows in a heart full of gratitude, and matures in the awe of His passionate love for us. Prayer is an act of humility because the person who prays acknowledges the need for Heaven's help and fellowship with the Creator. Prayerlessness is the ultimate pride. True humility understands its need for the Father. Humility also has eyes to see the awesome work our God has accomplished in the lives of others. We humble ourselves by helping others "have their day in the Son" while loving them with the same love we have for ourselves. Somebody once said, "The grace of God humbles a man without degrading him and exalts a man without inflating him!" We will see what practical humility looks like in the next chapter as we study its corollary royal attribute: honor.

Chapter 10

HONOR—THE YELLOW BRICK ROAD

Nobility grows in the soil of honor.

M Y mother's family is of Spanish descent and I spent a lot of time with them as I grew up. Honor was an integral part of our culture. My grandfather and grandmother were the eldest members of our family. They were the most respected people in any gathering that included them and the best seats in the house were always reserved for them. If one of the children sat in one of their seats, the rest of the family would just look over at them as if to say, "You can't be that rude!" We allowed the elderly to be served first and spoke to them with respect at all times, whether we agreed with them or not. We also always opened doors for women and gave them our seats. I can't remember anyone ever telling me to honor people, but I was born into a culture that modeled it.

Honor is a lost virtue in our nation. This fact was driven home to me at a Bethel School of Supernatural Ministry retreat. There were about 120 students present that weekend. Some of the students came over to my table late in the evening and began to ask questions. Within a few minutes about 30 students were huddled around the table while I told "war stories." They were all trying to participate in a very noisy conversation. A young man was sitting on the bench next to me. Later in the conversation, a middle-aged woman arrived. Finding no seat, she stood behind me so she could listen in on the conversation.

I said to the young man who was sitting next to me, "Please get up and let Julie sit there."

He snapped back, "I was here first!"

I said to him, "She's a woman; I want you to give up your seat for her." The tension rose for a moment, but he finally got up and gave her his seat.

This young man was one of our best students and has a great heart, but he was taught, "If you want a good seat, you need to get there early!" He was raised with a paradigm that valued "looking out for yourself" instead of honoring others. Thinking about honoring someone above himself hadn't entered into his equation. He had no grid for what I was sharing with him.

That young man is not alone. Honor has been almost completely removed from our culture. Many of you reading this book may struggle with this chapter for the same reason that the young man did not want to give up his seat. The whole idea that some people deserve more honor than others seems unfair. However, the kingdom mind-set is completely different than that. It's difficult to read the Bible without being exposed to a culture of submission with levels of honor and authority.

— HONOR JOINS THE GENERATIONS —

Honor has been absent from the Church's mind-set for so long that we often dishonor people when we minister without even realizing it. This became quite clear to me a few years ago. Over a period of 12 months, we had five different guest speakers come to Bethel Church and preach the message that "revival is coming from the youth." The first few times I heard that message my mind was troubled and my spirit was grieved, but I couldn't perceive what was wrong. As the end of the year approached, and a fifth speaker preached the same basic message again, I became upset and ran out of the church, weeping. (This isn't something I recommend pastors do.) I went home and lay on the floor, crying. I still didn't understand what was wrong so I began to question God about what was going on inside of me.

He told me, "Revival is not coming from the youth, but from ONE generation, *old to young.*" He reminded me of the passage in the Book of Acts that says, "It shall be in the last days, God says, that I will pour forth of My Spirit on all mankind; and your sons and your daughters shall prophesy, and your young men shall see visions and your old men shall dream dreams" (Acts 2:17). Take note that revival does not have a gender, a generation, or a social class. God went on to show me that every time the "youth message" was preached, the middle-aged and the elderly were being told, through omission, that they weren't important or valued anymore. He told me that the devil knew that he couldn't stop worldwide revival by resisting it, so he has tried to curse the planet by separating the generations.

The prophet Malachi saw this coming long ago and prophesied about it. Here is what he said about the last days:

> *Behold, I am going to send you Elijah the prophet before the coming of the great and terrible day of the Lord. He will restore the hearts of the fathers to their children and the hearts of the children to their fathers, so that I will not come and smite the land with a curse* (Malachi 4:5-6).

This passage makes it clear that as the generations join hands, the curses over our land will be broken. God went on to explain to me that the prince of the power of the air has influenced modern thought to value young people above the elderly in a way that dishonors older folks. The Lord showed me that the Bible intentionally gives more honor and respect to the elderly, but that our culture disempowers them. I began to understand that the wrong spirit was influencing many preachers and they were playing right into the hands of the evil one.

This point was magnified through a vision I had. In the vision I saw two young girls standing in the presence of their father on several different occasions. Every time their father saw the girls together he would tell one daughter that she was beautiful but never said anything to the other girl. The other daughter was being destroyed by her dad's lack of affection. I began to understand why I was carrying so much grief over the youth being honored five times in our house while in the presence of other generations. I also realized how destructive honor can be if it's abused.

— HONOR EXPRESSES VALUE IN OTHERS —

Honor is one of the greatest attributes of nobility in the entire Bible. When the kingdom is present inside us, honorable behavior comes naturally to us. We give honor to all men not just because they deserve it, but also because we are honorable citizens of the King. When we walk in our royal call, our behavior is not determined by our temporal environment but by the eternal environment that lies inside us.

Whenever we treat people honorably even if they refuse to honor us, we demonstrate that we have a standard within us that isn't determined by the people around us. We don't just honor people because they are honorable, we honor people because we are honorable. For a Christian, honor is a condition of the heart, not just the product of a good environment. Honor doesn't mean we agree with the people we are honoring; it simply means we value them as people who have been created in the image and likeness of God.

We should even fight with our enemy in an honorable way! We can see this principle in the Book of Jude:

> *Michael the archangel, when he disputed with the devil and argued about the body of Moses, did not dare pronounce against him a railing judgment, but said, "The Lord rebuke you!" But these men revile the things which they do not understand; and the things which they know by instinct, like unreasoning animals, by these things they are destroyed* (Jude 9-10).

If anyone deserves dishonor, it's the devil. But Michael didn't treat his archenemy with disrespect when he fought with him. This principle models how we should treat our enemies, whether physical or spiritual.

The war in Iraq presents a great example of this. When we discovered that several Iraqi prisoners were being mistreated in Iraq while being held as POWs, our country was shocked. As Americans, we couldn't tolerate this outrageous behavior. If those same Iraqi terrorists had been killed in battle, the citizens of the United States would have been far less outraged. We also know that when they capture our soldiers, they torture and behead them. So why is it wrong for us to torture them? The answer is simple: we want to deal with our enemies with honor not because they deserve it, but because we do. This is what it means to be honorable people.

— FAILURE OF HONOR IN LEADERSHIP —

Exodus 20:12 says, "Honor your mother and father so that your life will be prolonged." It is important to note the relationship between life and honor. Honor creates a highway on which life travels and it is a key virtue in creating and maintaining a royal culture. When we honor others, we recognize their authority and yield to their position. Honor is humility in action. It has eyes to see into the invisible in order to discern and appraise the nature of a person according to the values of the kingdom.

Honor is the cornerstone of an empowering culture that eliminates the need for control. The presence of honor creates order through dignity instead of the fear of punishment. Order, when it is fostered by honor, results in empowerment; order enforced through fear results in control. If we were to take negative consequences out of an environment where the people don't have honor in their hearts for one another, disorder and chaos would surely develop. People either obey their leaders because they are afraid of what might happen if they don't, or they do what is asked of them because they have honor in their hearts and respect those who have authority over them.

When honor erodes, death has an open door. The slow destruction of honor in our culture has not only caused our country's leadership to be disrespected, but it has also changed the way the church is governed.

In the last 50 years, America has been experiencing a foundational earthquake that has radically altered the leadership of our country. This cultural paradigm shift has far-reaching implications that stretch from the American family to the White House and from the business world to the Body of Christ. Throughout the last five decades, we have discovered that those whom we trusted most have lied, cheated, and stolen from us, often living lives of inconceivable immorality. At the same time, the morality of our families has also been eroding. This has resulted in the current generation being the most fatherless generation in the history of the world. These things have added up to a cultural mind-set of disrespect toward authority.

— Changing the Structure —

In response to the broken trust caused by those who have abused their authority, many churches have changed the structure of their administration instead of dealing with their leaders' hearts. Most churches in the last few decades have changed from a "rectangular table" of government to a "round table" of government. The rectangular table is a metaphor for a leadership structure that has levels of honor, while a round table describes a structure where each person has an equal say in church government. In a round table formation of leadership, the government of God has been replaced by church boards. These boards deem everyone equal and there is little or no ability to recognize the callings and anointings that rest on their leaders.

I should make it clear that I am not opposed to church boards. However, I am against governmental structures that react out of fear to the abuses of leadership and dishonor their senior leadership by taking away seats of honor. I do personally believe that in Christ everyone has an equal voice, but not everyone has an equal vote.

With round table leadership structure the overall emphasis is equality. It seeks to deal with the problems of the heart by taking away the opportunity for them to manifest. Changing the structure never touches the root issues, it is just another form of control. Therefore, no matter what the leadership structure is, abuse will happen. When we recreate a structure to cure a heart issue, the antidote is often worse than the disease.

In the Book of First Samuel 8, the elders of Israel changed their government structure instead of dealing with the issues of the heart. The elders of Israel had previous history dealing with Eli's sons who were both wicked. Eli was the judge who ruled over Israel before Samuel. At this point in the story, Eli and his sons were long gone and Samuel, who took Eli's place as judge, is about to die, so he appoints his two sons to rule over Israel. The problem is that Samuel's sons were also both wicked. The elders of Israel have a "been there, done that and seen the outcome" attitude. They do not want wicked people to rule over them again, so they ask for a king to rule instead of a judge.

On the surface, considering their options, it seems like they're making a noble request of Samuel. God's answer is almost stunning. He tells Samuel, "They have not rejected you but they have rejected me from being King over them" (1 Sam. 8:7). Was God saying that He didn't care that Samuel's sons were wicked and that they had permission to rule over Israel anyway? I don't think so. God was mad because they changed the leadership structure instead of dealing with the issues in their hearts. Samuel's sons needed to be confronted for their wickedness. Samuel and the elders should have removed them from leadership instead of changing their entire governmental system to avoid the conflict that confrontation causes.

The Shepherding Movement was probably one of the most dramatic and recent examples of abusive authority in the church. The cause of the abuse was that fatherly principles were given to elder brothers. Remember the attitude of the elder brother in the story of the prodigal son that we talked about earlier in this book? The elder brother said to his father, "You killed the fattened calf for him but you haven't even given me a goat."

His dad responded, "I killed the fattened calf for him, but you own the farm!" (see Luke 15:11-32).

So many leaders in the church today are more like the elder brother than the father in the story of the prodigal son. They believe lies about themselves, the Father, and their brothers, so they compete with the very people they're supposed to be leading. Still being paupers, their insecurity creates a desperate need to reinforce their power over their sons instead of empowering them.

True fathers honor their sons and desire to see their sons prosper and outgrow them. This elder brother attitude is what destroyed the Shepherding Movement. The leaders of the movement taught fatherly principles, but the recipients of the teaching were jealous and insecure. Many have refused to see that the problem was not so much the teaching but the misapplication of it as the result of unresolved heart problems in leaders. (There were other problems in the Shepherding Movement as well, but most of the problems were rooted in control.) Again, much like the elders of Israel in the days of Samuel, many have changed the structure instead of dealing with the issues of the heart.

— CHANGING THE HEART —

Instead of changing the system, Jesus taught us to change our hearts. At a dinner where people were scrambling for the seats of honor, He drew a stark contrast between their hearts and a heart of honor and humility that reflects God.

> *He began speaking a parable to the invited guests when He noticed how they had been picking out the places of honor at the table, saying to them, "When you are invited by someone to a wedding feast, do not take the place of honor, for someone more distinguished than you may have been invited by him, and he who invited you both will come and say to you, 'Give your place to this man,' and then in disgrace you proceed to occupy the last place. But when you are invited, go and recline at the last place, so that when the one who has invited you comes, he may say to you, 'Friend, move up higher'; then you will have honor in the sight of all who are at the table with you. For everyone who exalts himself will be humbled, and he who humbles himself will be exalted"* (Luke 14:7-11).

When the mother of the sons of Zebedee came to Jesus and asked if her sons could sit next to Him in His Kingdom, He said a position of honor in Heaven was not His to give, "but it is for those for whom it has been prepared by My Father" (Matt. 20:23). Throughout Scripture God tells us that He is, "opposed to the proud, but gives grace to the humble" (James 4:6).

Honor is humility in action. It is a matter of the heart and requires an honest assessment of the value of other people and a choice to focus on that above ourselves. As a friend of mine stated, "Arrogance isn't thinking too much of ourselves but thinking too little of others." If we want the grace God gives to the humble, we must put the wisdom of God into practice. "If anyone wants to be first, he shall be last of all and servant of all" (Mark 9:35).

This principle is foundational in the Kingdom of God. God is a God of honor, and the only way honor works is if there are levels of honor. It permits us to honor others above ourselves, and in doing so we permit God to honor us. It is because Jesus desires us to have honor that He teaches us how to humble ourselves and show honor to others. For this reason, when the mother of James and John asked for her sons to be honored, Jesus didn't say, "Oh, everyone sits at an equal distance from Me in Heaven." At dinner He didn't try to change the fact that there were levels of honor at the table.

God often describes people with the words "least" and "greatest." The government of Heaven is like a rectangular table. With this structure, we recognize that there are people who have been elevated above others and that they have something we need. Just as Elisha recognized he needed Elijah's mantle, so we have much to receive from those who have gone beyond us. In order to receive an inheritance and impartation from them, we need to have faith and expectation that they truly do have much to give. We show this by honoring them. Life flows from honoring them in our hearts.

God has ordained His structure of leadership with levels of honor because, as I've said, honor facilitates the flow of life in the Kingdom. When we change the structure we not only fail to fix the issues of the heart, we also prevent ourselves from receiving the benefits of life from godly leadership. Blaming and then abandoning the principles of God's Kingdom only destroys us and keeps us from His blessings.

Later we will discuss more about the leadership structure God designed for His body, but the point is that it is built on levels of honor which allow life to flow to every member as each person gives and receives the honor that is properly due.

— MAINTAINING A ROYAL CULTURE —

Since honor is such an important catalyst for life, we need to cultivate an attitude within us and a culture around us that promotes it. Nobility grows in the soil of honor. Learning to honor each other is vital to our growth in God.

A poor woman taught us about the extravagant manifestation of honor when she broke the alabaster vial and poured expensive perfume over Jesus' head. The disciples were indignant. They said, "This perfume might have been sold for a high price and the money given to the poor" (Matt. 26:9). Jesus reminded them that they always had the poor with them but He would be leaving them soon. Jesus then made a profound statement concerning this woman. He said, "Truly I say to you, wherever this gospel is preached in the whole world, what this woman has done will also be spoken of in memory of her."

Paupers know how to give when there's a need, but giving to those who don't have need seems like a waste to them. Jesus made it clear that royalty has a completely different value system. Princes give to honor people as well as to the needy.

This principle of honor is demonstrated every time we worship. We don't worship God because He needs our encouragement or anything else from us. Even though He deserves praise and worship, we worship Him out of honor and offer praise that He doesn't need.

In the same way, when kings, presidents, and prime ministers give gifts to one another, they will intentionally refrain from giving a gift that is needed. Giving to meet a need in another leader would be exposing a place of vulnerability in him, which would actually dishonor him. In other words, when we give to a leader something he needs we are saying that we have discovered a place of lack in his life. When we are fulfilling the need, we are actually saying, "We have something you don't have." Therefore, great leaders often exchange gifts that are luxuries to specifically honor each other.

The disciples did not have a perspective of honor in their hearts and it distorted their understanding of stewardship. They saw what the woman did for Jesus as a waste. Jesus said that her extravagant honor would make her famous. Honor will change the way we see the King and the manner in which we relate to His sons and daughters.

— EVANGELISM THROUGH HONOR —

Honor is also a powerful tool for evangelism. We only have as much influence in the lives of others as they have value for us. When we carry honor in our hearts for others, our value grows in their eyes and we gain a place of influence with them. Of course, when we honor in order to gain influence, it ceases to be honor. Honor must be in our hearts first, and it must be given freely. When we compliment people without honor in our hearts, our compliments feel like flattery to them. Americans are accustomed to being schmoozed by sales people who are trying to manipulate them into purchasing something. They can see right through their insincerity. But when we carry honor in our hearts people can feel it and their respect grows.

Judging and labeling groups of people usually promotes dishonor. Discrimination is an important subject in our society. In that sense we are a culture that is concerned with honor and respect, but because we've focused more on getting respect than giving it, honor hasn't been established. Intrinsic to honor is the ability to recognize people's individual characteristics and respect their power of choice. Empowerment means giving people what they need to make healthy choices.

Unfortunately, much of the church has been guilty of labeling everyone who doesn't know the Lord. The result is that often the only thing we see about people is the fact they don't know God. We jump in to address that need with our gospel "package" but turn people off because they feel that we only see them as pathetic and miss the rest of their individual value. If they believe we don't really value them as people, they won't believe we love them and will hold our offer suspect. Many evangelists have destroyed the Church's credibility by failing to demonstrate honor, which in turn earns the right to speak to someone.

What I am driving at is this: we've carried our picket signs in demonstrations, preached hellfire and brimstone on the corner of every major city in America, and boycotted major corporations in the name of God. We've ignored the simple truth of honor that literally transformed entire kingdoms in the days of Daniel and Joseph. Because Daniel and Joseph demonstrated honor to the pagan kings they served, both Pharaoh and Nebuchadnezzar eventually acknowledged the hand of God on their lives.

At Bethel Church, we have worked to honor everyone in our city, regardless of their religious persuasion. One example of our effort to honor people is the way we have shown the Native American community that we value them. A few years ago we had a service in which we invited the leaders of the local Native American tribe to come to church so we could repent for the way our forefathers sinned against their people. Most of the people in our local tribe don't know God yet, but they were deeply moved by our sincere love for them. As time passed the Lord began to talk to us about bringing forth fruit of our repentance. We invited the tribal leaders back to our church and gave them a $500-a-month honorarium to bless and honor them. We made a covenant with them that we would continue giving this money for as long as we remain leaders of Bethel Church.

The local tribe has come back to our church on several occasions to honor us with gifts. We have developed a great relationship with them and GOD IS MOVING AMONG THEIR TRIBE! We are seeing firsthand how God designed life to flow through our honor.

Life flows through honor. I pray that we gain understanding of how to honor God and all people in this world, regardless of age, religious background, or persuasion.

Chapter 11

ROYALTY IS DYING TO BE TOGETHER

Judas wanted intimacy without covenant; that's why he left supper during communion and then betrayed Jesus with a kiss.

— BORN INTO A FAMILY —

FOR some, the word *royalty* may inspire images of the kings of old who used their endless wealth and power to fulfill their wanton pleasure through their harems filled with concubines. Concubines cohabited with the king without covenant. Therefore their children didn't carry the king's name, nor did they receive any inheritance.

Our King has no concubines! He is a righteous and holy King who teaches His sons and daughters that passion must only be expressed inside the boundaries of purity and that children are to be the fruit of covenant relationships.

People who are lost in darkness need more than a power encounter with God for true and lasting change to take place in their lives. They need a relationship with the Lord and His people. The power of God delivers us out of the clutches of the devil, destroys the disease of sin and thrusts us into the Kingdom of His beloved Son as a newborn child of God. The born-again experience is only the beginning of life as a new creation, and that life requires nurturing and care from the family of God for it to grow. Obviously the same is true of natural birth, which is why, from the very beginning of time, God intended children to be the fruit of a loving, passionate relationship between a husband and wife.

The Bible says, *"Adam knew Eve his wife; and she conceived and bore Cain"* (Gen. 4:1 NKJV). The word "knew" here in the Hebrew does not mean sexual intercourse. The Bible assumes that you understand that Cain was not conceived through immaculate conception. Rather, the word "knew" is the Hebrew word *yada*. It means to have a deep, intimate relationship with someone. God is saying that Adam had a deep personal relationship with Eve, and out of that place of intimacy, Cain was conceived.

God fashioned the blood covenant right into nature itself. For years scientists have been bewildered over what purpose the hymen plays in the body of a woman. It seems to have no physical reason for being there. When it is broken it does not heal like every other part of the body. One day I realized that God only wants children to be born out of a covenant relationship between a husband and wife, therefore He provided the blood so that the covenant could be ratified before the children were conceived.

In our society, it has become commonplace for children to be conceived from a one-night stand or a brush with passion. Worse yet, some children are the product of a rape. Rape occurs when one person forces their will upon another. We live in a culture that desires intimacy without responsibility and pleasure without covenant. We'll look more at the fruit of that desire in a moment, but I want to point out that unknowingly, much of the Church has been influenced by this mind-set. Week after week we see people born again at our altars. But where are they? Most of them, not long after they weep in repentance, are thrust into a struggle for survival.

None of this comes close to mirroring God's plan, which is for new believers not just to be applauded as they are going forward to the altar, but also to be received by a family who will personally feed and lead them. The worldly culture has helped create a strange mentality in some of the Church. We think nothing of people being born from a night of "passion," only to be left at our altars with a prayer they don't understand and a Bible they can't read.

— MY OWN COVENANTS —

I will never forget the night that Kathy and I received the Lord. I was 18 and Kathy was 15 years old at the time.

I had an encounter three years earlier that sent me on a journey to find God. My mother had become very sick with psoriasis and her body was covered with a rash. To make matters worse, for nearly a year we had a prowler looking through our windows at night and terrorizing us. One night I even took a shot at him after I awoke to find him coming through my bedroom window.

The police were at our house several times a week. My mother was sleeping on the couch with a shotgun. I would wake up in the middle of the night and hear my mom crying as she struggled to keep herself together. This was all extremely unsettling for a 15-year-old boy who was the oldest of three children. We were not raised in a religious home and therefore I didn't really know if there was a God. One summer night, at about three o'clock in the morning, the pressure got to be too much for me. I sat up against my headboard. It was pitch dark and I could hear my mother weeping quietly in the front room.

I cried out in desperation, "If there is a God, if you heal my mother, I will find out who you are and I will serve you the rest of my life!"

An audible voice answered, "My name is Jesus Christ and you have what you requested!"

The next morning my mother woke up completely healed. Her psoriasis was gone! Within a few days the police caught the prowler and life began to change.

A week or so passed and I was lying on my bed around midnight contemplating these amazing events when the voice spoke to me again.

He said, "My name is Jesus Christ. You said if I healed your mother you would serve me and I am waiting!"

I began searching for God everywhere. I would go to different churches and stand in the back during the service and wait to see if God was there. I would often leave in disappointment saying to myself, "The

God who spoke to me isn't here." Finally, three years later, Kathy and I were invited to a friend's fellowship. It was a home group packed with young people. They were all excited about Jesus. We came in and sat down on the floor with about a hundred other kids. The worship started and everyone began to sing passionately with their hands raised. As the music died down, the leader gave an invitation for anyone who wanted to receive Christ. Kathy and I raised our hands and prayed a prayer asking the Lord to forgive our sins and come into our lives.

We didn't realize it then, but what happened next would forever change our lives. After the meeting ended the leader came over and introduced himself. He explained what it meant to be saved, how we were newborn babies in the kingdom and we needed to be fathered. He then introduced us to three young men and asked which one of those men we wanted to "father" us. I didn't realize that "fathering" wasn't normal in church at that time because I hadn't been in church much. We picked a man named Art Kipperman who was about three years our senior. He and his wife, Cathy, became our spiritual parents. It was awesome having someone to mentor us and speak into our lives. We had a relationship with them from that point on.

A few years later we moved up to the Trinity Alps in northern California. We lived there a year without the benefit of having a spiritual father and mother living alongside us. I was starving to be nurtured and felt lost. I began to cry out for God to send me a father.

I was working as a mechanic in a repair shop at the time. One day while I was laying on a creeper underneath a green Jeep Wagoneer the Lord spoke to me saying, "The man who owns this Jeep will be your father." I had been praying fervently that day about the void in my life, but I didn't even know the man who owned the Jeep.

When that particular customer came in to pick up his vehicle I collected his money and explained the work order to him. I was so nervous. He was about twenty years older than me and seemed very warm and loving. I accompanied him to his car, still trying to gather the courage to tell him what God had said to me. He got in the Jeep and rolled down his window as I stumbled over my words.

Finally I blurted out, "God told me that the man who owed this Jeep would be my spiritual father!" (I was choking back tears.) He turned off the engine and opened the door of his truck. He stood up, wrapped his arms around me and said, "I would be honored to be your father!" This man's name is Bill Derryberry and he has been my mentor for more than 20 years. His love and discipline have changed my life. I am forever indebted to him.

The love that Bill and I have for each other has resulted in many people being born into the Kingdom through both Bill's encouragement in my own life and the contagious nature of love when it is expressed through someone. In the same way, God's desire is for the bride and the bridegroom to be so passionately in love with one another that children are the natural outcome. The very presence of our children reminds us of the covenant love that we share. When conceived in love rather than lust, the natural outgrowth of children and their parents is an unbreakable, unchangeable and everlasting bond. Their children's hearts become tablets on which husbands and wives write their love letters to one another. The outcome of this kind of relationship is that the children are secure, well-adjusted and have a healthy self-worth because their parents value them.

When the Church of Jesus becomes a family instead of a harem, people won't just come to church, they will become the church. It will no longer be a place they go to but a tribe they live in, a people they have responsibility for and a family that nurtures one another in good times and in bad, in sickness and health, until death do us part. They won't change churches just because the worship isn't as good as Joe's Super Church down the street. They will be committed to a family where they hear the voice of their Shepherd in the people who are leading them.

Covenant also means that people belong to a fellowship to be a contributor rather than a consumer. Covenant breaks the back of the pressure that leaders feel to perform because their flock hasn't come to be entertained but they have come to be led.

— THE FATHERLESS GENERATION —

We live in what is probably one of the most fatherless generations in the history of the world. This is due in part to people opting for cohabitation and divorce rather than committed relationships. Even people who get married in America are often more concerned about making a buck than nurturing a family. Yet there remains a promise from long ago that an old prophet best articulates in his vision of the future. As I said before,

> *Behold, I am going to send you Elijah the prophet before the coming of the great and terrible day of the Lord. He will restore the hearts of the fathers to their children and the hearts of the children to their fathers, so that I will not come and smite the land with a curse* (Malachi 4:5-6).

Almost 3,000 years ago, the prophet Malachi knew the importance of reuniting fathers and sons in the last days. He saw the restoration of covenant relationships as the force that would shatter the curses of our land. This last days' revival will be founded in both the natural and spiritual family.

Curses are the powerful and the painful cost of absent and broken covenants. I know this firsthand, as I shared with you in the first chapter. After the death of my father, my mom gave birth to my little brother Kelly, the son of my first stepfather. Their marriage disintegrated when Kelly was five years old. After their divorce, Kelly's dad would call, drunk, about once a month to exercise his visiting rights.

He would say, "I'm going to pick up Kelly at five o'clock tonight." Kelly would be so excited to go see his dad that he would be packed early in the morning. He would take his little suitcase and sit out on the front porch, usually an hour or two early. He would sit there hour after hour, whether he was in the blazing hot sun or in the freezing cold winter. He would wait outside late into the night.

I would finally come out and say, "Kelly, why don't you come in now? Your dad must not be coming."

But he would say, "My dad is coming. I know he's coming!"

Usually around midnight he would fall asleep on top of his little suitcase. I would pick him up and carry him to bed. This pattern continued for years, resulting in deep wounds and a broken heart. Out of necessity, children who survive in this environment become independent and rebellious because they have learned that they cannot trust people, especially those who have authority over them.

There are so many Kellys in the world who are either born outside of covenant, or experience their parents breaking covenant through divorce. There are many other children who have moms and dads that parent as a hobby or as a side job because they are out chasing "success." When loving relationships are absent in the lives of children, another message is written on their hearts, which is not love, but rather rejection and abandonment. These things get carved into their tender little hearts through reckless words and lonely nights.

The same condition is prominent in the Kingdom. Much like my little brother who was not fathered, we in the Church have given birth to children and then left them fatherless and trying to survive on their own. Jesus never intended for us to make Christians but rather to make disciples. The word *disciple* means "learner." The very nature of a disciple is that they need someone to teach them.

What happens to the new believers who are not parented? Most of them go back into the world from which they came. Later when someone tries to win them back to Christ, it is nearly impossible. They think, "I've already tried that and it didn't work." The truth of the matter is that what they experienced has little to do with the gospel. The gospel means "good news." A large part of the "good" that's in the "news" is that we were all supposed to be born into a family that cared for us, not just be influenced by fanatical people who cared mostly about winning souls rather than adopting sons and daughters.

Much like a woman who gets pregnant on a date, we lead people to Christ without any relationship or plan to parent them. This often happens in our services. We let the music create the right atmosphere for romance. The preacher has practiced his lines because he's used them many times before; the passion grows and then the child is conceived. Sometimes it's more like a forced rape, where we scare people into the Kingdom by telling them about all the bad things that will happen to them if they don't come forward or raise their hand right then! (The way evangelism is taught in many circles today reminds me more of a sales clinic than a Lamaze class. These people care more about getting someone to pray a prayer than they are concerned about how to pre- parc for children to born.) When children are conceived this way, they are bastards (see Heb. 12:8 KJV). They don't even know who their father is. In our intoxication we told them that we love them. But too often, we never show it. Too often, no one ever picks them up! We cannot allow this perversion of the gospel to continue. We must rise up and become fathers and mothers who care. The Kellys of the world are wait- ing for someone to be a parent to them.

In the last hundred years, through the birth of the Pentecostal Movement, we have witnessed the restoration of the Holy Spirit's min- istry in and through the Church. In the late 1960s and early 1970s we saw the Jesus Movement completely alter the hippie culture and trans- form many of our cities. This last revival will be initiated by the prophets and will emphasize the ministry of the Father. It will be typified by the complete reformation and restoration of fatherhood and sonship. As it revolutionizes the family unit it will ultimately transform our culture.

— True Covenant —

Fatherhood begins with marriage. Marriage is initiated through covenant. Covenant is comprised of three facets. First, it means an agree- ment that is only to be broken by death. Second, the nature of a covenant is that those who make it die to themselves for the sake of their covenant partner; and last, people who are in covenant give each other the right to influence their decisions. In other words, the focus of each member of the covenant is, "I'm in this relationship for what I can give to it, not just for what I can receive from it."

A cohabiting relationship says, "I'm in this relationship for what I can get from you. Therefore, I am only in this relationship for as long as you please me." People who live together without being married often excuse themselves by saying that marriage is just a piece of paper. The truth of the matter is that the intentional lack of commitment creates a fear in one partner that the other will leave, motivating them to do whatever they can to keep the other pleased. In their codependency the couple doesn't want to make an agreement that lasts forever because that will take away the element of insecurity that they use to keep their partner under pressure to perform.

Those who cohabit find it very difficult to make a decision to be committed to someone forever because they have very little control over how someone else will treat them in the future. In a covenant relationship, it is easier to make a lifetime commitment because "I am in it for what I can give to the relationship and I have complete control over my own behavior."

God is a covenant-making being. He made a covenant with man that was based on man's ability to be righteous through keeping rules (the Old Testament and Covenant). Later, God wanted to change the covenant that he had made with man, but a covenant is terminated only by death. Therefore, God, as Jesus Christ, had to die so that he could change the agreement, as Paul describes in Romans and Galatians.

Although many Christians were raised in a "cohabiting" church culture where people didn't commit, leaders were controlling or people pleasing, and true discipleship was lacking, the truth of the matter is that when we receive Christ, we come into a covenant relationship with God and His people. Water baptism is the prophetic act that initiates this covenant. According to Romans chapter six, when we go underwater in baptism, it is a prophetic declaration that we are being buried with Christ in death. When we come up out of the water, we are demonstrating that our life is now found in Christ who raised us from the dead (see Rom. 6:3-11). "It is no longer I who live but Christ who lives in me" (Gal. 2:20).

Keeping covenant with God is the mark of a true disciple. Jesus had 12 apostles. He kept saying that one of them would betray him. It is a little scary to me that the 11 other guys who lived, slept, ate and ministered together in power for three-and-a-half years still had not realized that Judas was a betrayer. Judas must have been able to heal the sick and cast out demons as well as any of the other disciples, because otherwise his lack of power would have been a dead giveaway that he was the betrayer. Then, on the night of the Passover, Jesus basically said, "Let's make a covenant." He took bread and said, "This is my body that is broken for you" (Luke 22:19). As soon as Judas realized that covenant was required, his cover was blown.

Judas was a false apostle. He betrayed Jesus with a kiss because he pursued intimacy without covenant (see Luke 22:47). He was in relationship with Jesus for what he could get out of it. When he realized that Jesus was about to require him to sacrifice himself for the sake of Christ, he sold out what was left of his stock in Christ for 30 pieces of silver. He didn't want to be in a relationship that cost him.

The nature of false apostles and false leaders is that they are not really fathers. They cohabitate with the Body for what they can get out of them. The children that they reproduce are incidental. They never plan to take care of them. When they finally get caught in their own sin, they try to create their own redemption (Judas hung himself) instead of receiving what Christ did for them.

As I mentioned, this Judas spirit is very prominent in our culture. It has begun to dominate the mind-set of our country and is exemplified in so many ways, both in the church and out of it. It is so important that we, as princes and princesses, refuse to allow the spirit of our day to influence us but instead operate in the opposite spirit.

Many years ago the Lord convicted me of the cohabiting attitude that I had toward Bill Johnson. Bill has been my senior leader and pastor for more than a quarter of a century. He is one of the most amazing men I have ever known and I have a deep respect for him. One night the Lord revealed my heart toward Bill. Although I had served him well and had done my best for him, I never had any intention of staying with him forever. I wanted to be the Man, the Boss, the number one guy and I was using Bill to get there. The Lord said to me, "You're always talking about covenant but you haven't made one with your senior father! You are serving him to benefit yourself, not for his benefit. I want you dedicate the rest of your life to serving him."

Wow! I was undone. I realized then how much I didn't want to be in submission to someone. All my trust issues began to surface. Did I really believe that if I gave my life to serve Bill that he would reciprocate the relationship? More importantly, did I trust that Jesus could give me the desires of my heart while I was the servant of another man? Could I live with Bill getting credit for things that I accomplished because people saw Bethel as "Bill's church"? Did I want to spend my entire life living in the shadow of a famous man? My false heart was unmasked. Yuck, Yuck, Yuck!

The conviction grew day by day until I could no longer stand it. I couldn't just have a message, I had to *be* the message. I needed to make a change in my life but it was a battle.

Bill and I were doing a men's retreat together in Orangevale, California, right at the height of my tension. It was tough, and to make matters worse we were riding in the same car together all the way there. On the way there we hardly talked which isn't unlike Bill (he is very quiet), yet it was a minor miracle for me. I was afraid to talk because I wasn't sure what might jump out of my mouth. Finally I couldn't take it any longer. Bill was driving and I looked over at him and I blurted out, "I covenant to spend the rest of my life serving you. One of the main goals of my life from this day on is to make sure that you accomplish all that God has given you to do with your life and I will stay with you until I die."

I thought I was going to pass out, because I had such a deep revelation of what I had just done and I am a man who keeps my word. Bill glanced over at me and said, "Thanks." I think Bill thought I was verbalizing something I had always carried in my heart because I had served him for so long, but that wasn't the case. Those words have changed my life. I have come into a whole new level in God since then. My ministry has exploded and my finances have more than doubled. In fact, this book is a result of Bill encouraging and promoting me. He even called Destiny Image and arranged for them to read my manuscript.

This transition from concubine to covenant must take place so the Church once again can be "The Family of God." The mark of true royalty is the ability to lay down our lives in covenant with others for the sake of the Kingdom. As the Church truly becomes a family and gives birth to sons and daughters, expressing the covenant we have with the Bridegroom, the foundations of our cities will be rocked. This will cause a dramatic contrast between the world's lust and God's love! At last the world will receive what it is longing for…the supernatural, unconditional love of the Father who loves us as sons and daughters. It's about time that we give them the real thing!

Chapter 12

DEFENDING THE DECREES
OF THE KING

Royal people have a powerful sense of justice in the depths of their souls compelling them to action when they come upon injustice.

— HEROES OF JUSTICE —

WE'VE seen how God has called us to glory and how true humility and honor are vital attributes for carrying that glory properly. Humility and honor are sustained by understanding and maintaining a heart of covenant love for God and each other. Bill Johnson says, "You can tell what a person loves by what he hates." God loves His children, He is jealous for them and hates anything that violates love. He calls it injustice. As we grow in His heart for one another and for the world, we begin as royalty to develop a hatred for injustice and a deeply rooted drive to see it undone.

Let's look at the need for justice in a few of the characters we've studied in this book. If you remember, Moses always knew he was a Hebrew but grew up as a prince in Pharaoh's house. He was raised in an environment where the contrast between his situation and that of his people was in his face. One day he sees two of his brothers being mistreated by an Egyptian and takes action (see Exod. 2:11-12). What caused Moses to defend his brothers? Why didn't he just hang out in the palace and watch movies? Why do people who "have it made" mess up their comfort zone to stand up for some poor soul who is being abused?

Most people know the difference between right and wrong. But royal people have a powerful sense of justice in the depths of their souls that drives them to act when they see something wrong. In the same way that Moses could not help but do something when he saw his brothers being mistreated, the sons and daughters of the king are driven to right injustice, destroy evil, and see righteousness prevail in the world.

We can see how this sense of justice moves royal people to action in Acts 17 when the apostle Paul arrives in Athens. Initially, his purpose there was to hang out and wait for Silas and Timothy, but when he saw that the city was worshiping false gods, he got stirred up. Verse 16 says that his spirit was "provoked within him as he observed the idols of Athens." He began teaching in the marketplace and got enough attention that the people had him preach at the Areopagus, where all the leading teachers and philosophers of the day spoke. His pursuit of justice ended up winning him a platform to tell the whole city about Jesus.

While Paul was provoked by what he saw going on in Athens, Gideon was a man who became provoked by what *wasn't* going on in Israel. Before we meet Gideon in Judges 6, let me describe the historical setting. The Midianites, Amalekites and the armies of the east were oppressing his country. The Lord had already sent a prophet to remind the Israelites of their history with the God of Heaven, and how He freed them from Egyptian oppression using powerful signs and wonders.

Unfortunately, no such deliverance had come for Israel yet. As a result, we meet Gideon hiding in a winepress, trying to save the wheat crop from the enemy who came at harvest to destroy the fields. An Angel of the Lord came to him with this great proclamation: "The Lord is with you, O valiant warrior." Gideon's response was stunning. He said, "O my lord, if the Lord is with us, why then has all this happened to us? And where are all His miracles which our fathers told us about, saying, 'Did not the Lord bring us up from Egypt?' But now the Lord has abandoned us and given us into the hand of Midian" (Judg. 6:12-13).

Gideon was tired of hiding in the winepress beating out wheat. (Have you ever been sick and tired of being sick and tired?) He had been hearing the prophet's reminder of all Israel had seen God do, and he wanted to know why there was such a huge gap between the miraculous works of the past and Israel's utter powerlessness to change their present circumstances. Like us, he wanted to know why there was such a distance between what the Bible said there should be and what he was actually experiencing. Royalty cannot live with this incongruity in their hearts. There is a passion that lies in our souls that causes us to rise up and confront the injustice of our day. This passion was boiling under the surface of Gideon's soul, waiting for an opportunity and encouragement from the Lord in order to act.

It's great to hang out in the palace and enjoy all the benefits of being the King's kids, but the more we begin to walk in our royal identity, the more we are going to find something rising in us when we are exposed to injustice. For many of us, the need for justice has been disempowered by false beliefs we've embraced in the midst of unresolved injustices we've experienced. But as we encounter God's faithfulness in our own lives, we will find ourselves provoked to action.

We see King Saul's royal identity emerging through exposure to injustice in the Book of First Samuel. Saul was anointed king of Israel, but directly after his anointing ceremony, instead of leading Israel, he went back to what was familiar to him and worked on his farm. After all, he grew up as a pauper and not a prince. He didn't know what it looked like to rule. Israel had never had a king, so there were no role models to guide him in his new position. Not much time passed before he heard word from the elders of the city of Jabesh Gilead about how they were going to be losing their right eyes to the Ammonites in order to make a peace treaty with them (see 1 Sam. 11:1-5). What the prophet Samuel began in Saul's life by anointing him king suddenly came to fruition when he encountered injustice. Here is the Bible's account of what happened:

> *Now Nahash the Ammonite came up and besieged Jabesh-gilead; and all the men of Jabesh said to Nahash, "Make a covenant with us and we will serve you."*

But Nahash the Ammonite said to them, "I will make it with you on this condition, that I will gouge out the right eye of every one of you, thus I will make it a reproach on all Israel."

The elders of Jabesh said to him, "Let us alone for seven days, that we may send messengers throughout the territory of Israel. Then, if there is no one to deliver us, we will come out to you." Then the messengers came to Gibeah of Saul and spoke these words in the hearing of the people, and all the people lifted up their voices and wept.

Now behold, Saul was coming from the field behind the oxen, and he said, "What is the matter with the people that they weep?"

So they related to him the words of the men of Jabesh. Then the Spirit of God came upon Saul mightily when he heard these words, and he became very angry. He took a yoke of oxen and cut them in pieces, and sent them throughout the territory of Israel by the hand of messengers, saying, "Whoever does not come out after Saul and after Samuel, so shall it be done to his oxen." Then the dread of the Lord fell on the people, and they came out as one man (1 Samuel 11:1-7).

Many in the Body of Christ are in the same state Saul was in before he encountered injustice. We have been anointed as kings and priests, we have been commanded to disciple nations, and we have been equipped with the wisdom, power, and authority of God Himself. Yet somehow, we find ourselves following some silly oxen around the farm, going back to our old habits and focusing on survival when we've been called to lead and influence people for the Kingdom.

However, injustice has a way of drawing out the royal call in our lives. We can always tell how much of our princely identity we are truly walking in by our response to injustice: either our spirits get provoked within us, driving us to act, or we run for cover.

— A JUSTICE OF RESTORATION —

It is the most natural thing in the world for God's royal family (us) to care about justice. The Psalmist wrote, "Righteousness and justice are the foundation of His throne" (Ps. 97:2b). Those who live with His throne in their hearts are moved to bring righteousness and justice into every situation.

Our Elder Brother, Jesus, came to earth to deal with sin, the root of injustice, once and for all on the cross. He modeled for us what bringing justice looks like. Interestingly, He didn't go around punishing people for their sins. Many people think justice looks like people getting the punishment they deserve. That's only one side of justice, and it is important to realize that it has already been dealt with. Jesus Himself fulfilled the demand of justice by taking the penalty for our sin on the cross. He took what we deserved, and through faith, we have access to the life He deserved.

Jesus described the justice He came to bring in Luke 4:18-19 NKJV:

> *The Spirit of the Lord is upon me, because He has anointed me to preach the gospel to the poor; He has sent me to heal the brokenhearted, to proclaim liberty to the captives and recovery of sight to the blind, to set at liberty those who are oppressed; to proclaim the acceptable year of the Lord.*

Jesus' justice is a justice of restoration. It gives back to people that which sin took from them. When the Bible says, "The wages of sin is death," it's not just talking about when our bodies stop functioning and are put in the ground. Death is the spiritual condition of being separated from God, and the death of the body is the result of that separation. The Bible tells us that we're already dead in sin when we're born into this world. This death is at work in and around us during our whole life on earth. It doesn't only affect our final end, but our entire quality of life on the planet.

Sin causes all sorts of problems for us in every area of our life. It affects our health, our relationships, our finances, our minds, and our emotions. The amazing thing is that Jesus' death didn't just make it possible for us to go to Heaven when we die, but to live with all the benefits of a restored relationship with our Father right now. He made it possible for every effect of sin in our lives to be reversed. Because He took the punishment of our sin, we don't have to live with sickness, poverty, broken relationships, emotional pain, or mental torment. All of that was covered and rendered powerless by the blood of Jesus.

We are partnering with God to bring justice to the earth. It reverses every effect of sin and death in people's lives because it is the justice of restoration. Like Paul, we are restoring the knowledge of the one true God. Like Gideon, we are restoring the supernatural signs of God. We're restoring health to people's bodies, souls, and spirits. We're restoring relationships and families. We're restoring financial prosperity. We're restoring morality in the government. We're restoring holiness in the arts. We're restoring the land and much more.

We still haven't seen all the effects of sin reversed in the world around us because the power of the Cross is only accessed through faith. Faith sees the finished work of the Cross in eternity and contends to see it released in history. We have to contend for it because there is resistance. This resistance comes from the fact that, as Second Corinthians 4:3-4 (NKJV) says, "Our gospel…is veiled to those who are perishing, whose minds the god of this age has blinded, who do not believe, lest the light of the gospel of the glory of Christ, who is the image of God, should shine on them." We have an enemy who comes to steal, kill, and destroy. He works through deception, and those who believe his lies empower him and his kingdom of darkness to keep sin and death in their lives.

The truth is that Christ defeated and disarmed the enemy once and for all on the Cross (see Col. 2:15). God has condemned him as guilty and handed over the authority he had usurped from Adam to Jesus Christ, the second Adam. Our job as "little Christs" is as deputies who enforce that judgment in every situation we come across. God created a world where our vote counts and where our agreement with what He's doing is necessary to release His power into the world. He did this so He wouldn't violate our free will and ruin our potential to love Him from our hearts.

Jesus demonstrated what can happen when one person totally agrees with the will of the Father. His ministry didn't cause the whole world to be evangelized or saved in His lifetime. Instead, He equipped a small group of disciples to bring justice to whatever situation in which they found themselves. Then, through His death, He made that power available to any who would believe. He set it up so that the knowledge of the glory of God could only cover the earth as each believer takes responsibility where they are to, "Do justly, to love mercy, and to walk humbly with his God" (Mic. 6:8 NKJV).

Isaiah (chapters 59–61) speaks of the justice that God brought to the earth through Christ and what He also desires to extend through His Body.

— TRUE SPIRITUAL POWER —

Unfortunately, when much of the Church looks at the world, they see the enemy's kingdom from a defensive position. A lot of us in the Church are intimidated by the Goliaths of our day: the giants of crime, pornography, false religion and other evils that mock the armies of the living God. We are just trying to hold on until the rapture takes us out of the war zone. Our desire to do something about injustice gets buried by our fear.

One of the reasons many Christians have felt powerless in the face of injustice is that they lack training in their identity and ability to wage spiritual warfare. But the way in which the Kingdom of God is established must also be understood. Jesus told the Pharisees in Luke 11:20 (NKJV), "But if I cast out demons with the finger of God, surely the kingdom of God has come upon you." When the Kingdom of God comes, it always displaces the kingdom of darkness.

As Ephesians 6:12 (NKJV) reminds us, "For we do not wrestle against flesh and blood, but against principalities, against powers, against the rulers of the darkness of this age, against the spiritual hosts of wickedness in the heavenly places." This means that while our national government addresses injustice by means of court trials and waging physical wars, the Church addresses the roots of injustice in the spiritual realm.

When we look at the darkness of our cities and nation, we understand that locking criminals behind bars won't satisfy justice. Justice will only come when the Kingdom of God displaces the spiritual hosts of wickedness in the heavenly realms.

The world is waiting to see true spiritual power, and until the Church rises up to demonstrate the power of the Kingdom, they (the world) will be held under the power of darkness. The Church must allow God to position us for confrontations with the kingdom of darkness, as He did when He sent Elijah to Jezebel and Moses to Pharaoh. Both of these men demonstrated the power of God in Israel in such a way that they were forced to recognize that Yahweh was the true God and would vindicate those true to Him.

Elijah, followed by his servant Elisha, traveled throughout the world ravaging the powers of darkness and wreaking havoc on evil kingdoms. When God famously brought down fire on Elijah's altar in a dramatic confrontation on Mount Carmel, he overcame 850 false prophets of Baal and Asherah. Neither of these men had tolerance for the destructive behavior of wicked kings, but rather turned many to righteousness. They raised the dead, healed the sick, destroyed false prophets, and saw revival spread through their land. They were feared by many and respected by all. They walked in great purity and God was their friend.

It is time for the Body of Christ to rise up and receive our inheritance! We must rid ourselves of complacency and restore the ancient boundaries of holiness and demonstrations of great power. We can't be satisfied with illustrated sermons, great music, or friendly services. We have been called to see the powers of darkness destroyed and our ruined cities restored.

Wickedness continues to grow all around us, taking root in the lives of those we love and eroding the very foundation of our country. Satanism is spreading like wildfire. Psychics laugh in the face of the church as they demonstrate the power of the dark side. Divorce is destroying our families and violence, our children. Cancer and other dreaded diseases take the lives of so many. Yet the words of our Lord Jesus still echo through the halls of history, "These signs will follow those who believe," and "Greater works shall you do because I go to the Father" (Mark 16:17-18; John 14:12).

During Moses' day, God demonstrated His power to Pharaoh. Pharaoh counter-attacked by having his sorcerers duplicate the miracles of God. Then the God of Heaven, who has all power, performed *extraordinary* miracles so that even the sorcerers said, "This must be God. We cannot perform these miracles" (Exod. 8:19, paraphrased). Finally Pharaoh was overcome by God's power and let His people go.

Pharaoh is a metaphoric example of satan, who is being forced to let go of his demonic stronghold on our cities as God demonstrates His raw power through His church. We are in the midst of the greatest revival in human history. Yet there remains a distance between what *should* be and what *will* be. That distance is us! What will *we* be? We are the bridge between *history* and *His story*. We are *the sons of the prophets!* The sick, the demonized, the poor, the blind, the lame, and the lost are all waiting to see what we have learned. We can't afford to disappoint them!

— PERSONAL EMPOWERMENT —

One of the ways we displace darkness and bring the Kingdom of God is by each of us, as His children, using the gifts with which we have been equipped. We don't always realize that these gifts are not just tools for strengthening the Body, but weapons for waging warfare. In December 1999, the Lord led me into an encounter that revealed how the prophetic gift He had given me had power to fight. The utter bondage the world lives in was driven home in my heart through this experience. It convinced me that it will only be undone through the raw power of God being demonstrated like He did through Moses and Elijah.

I was invited to speak at a state university on the subject of "Christianity and the Supernatural." A pastor in the area, who pastors a church near the campus, had begun teaching a class at the university to expose the students to the power of God. Several students from our own ministry school as well as some of our staff members were with us that day.

The air was charged with excitement as we walked toward the campus. On the way there, the pastor described the class to me:"There will be twenty-one students in the class.Ten of them are Christians, three of them are into witchcraft, and the rest of them belong to religions that you probably could not pronounce." It was a good thing I hadn't known what I was getting myself into until that moment, because if I had, I probably wouldn't have agreed to do it. I hadn't realized I was about to address a class full of intelligent college students, some of whom were participating in witchcraft. (My higher educational experience consisted of attending "What's A-Matter U" and graduating with a degree in "Hammerology." I've never been beyond high school.) Fear began to fill my heart as we reached the campus.

Just as we passed through the back door, I heard the Lord say to me, "I am going to show off today!"

"Show off?" I thought."Is that in the Bible? Lord, is that you?" I asked. Before I could receive an answer, I was being introduced to the class.

I began to tell the students about my life and how the Lord had delivered me from a three-and-a-half-year-long nervous breakdown. Even though I was a Christian during those three years, I shook so badly every day that I couldn't get a glass of water to my face without using two hands. At night, I would sweat so heavily that the bed would be completely soaked. Kathy often would get up two or three times a night just to change our sheets.The last year of my breakdown was pure hell. Demons began to visit me and tormented me until I became demonized.The Lord finally delivered me.As I told my story, the students were hanging on every word.

The campus leader of wicca, a form of witchcraft, was in the class. Suddenly, the Lord gave me a prophetic word for him.

I asked him, "Would you please stand up?" Reluctantly and almost defiantly, he stood to his feet. I continued, "The Lord showed me that you have been called to politics. God has blessed you with the ability to understand political matters. This has been in your heart since you were a little boy. Come forward and let me pray for you."

Sitting down, he said, "No way!" My anxiety level grew again, but I decided to press in and go on.

I talked a bit more, and then the pastor signaled for me to wrap up. As I made my way out of the class, students gathered around and began asking me all kinds of questions.

A young lady from the back of the room said, "I'm supposed to talk to you."

"Are you a Christian?" I asked.

"No!" she said. "But I know I am supposed to talk to you." She pushed her way through the crowd to the front of the room.

I said to her, "Your mother was a psychic, wasn't she?"

"Yes," she replied.

I added, "You think that you are a psychic, but you have been called to be a prophetess."

"That's right!" she exclaimed.

"There has been an evil spirit assigned to kill you since you were born, and as a matter-of-fact, you almost died at birth," I continued.

She looked shocked. "Yes!" she yelled out. "Yes! Yes! That's exactly right! I did nearly die at birth and there has been a demon trying to kill me ever since I was born. It came into my room the other night and tried to run over me" (I can't imagine what that must have looked like), "but I stood up on my bed and said, 'The blood of Jesus sets me free,' and it left!"

Evidently, the class had just studied the power in the blood of Jesus that very week. For some reason, even though she wasn't a Christian, the demon had left her.

The pastor saw that another class was attempting to enter the room, so he said, "Come on, we need to get out of here."

I said to the girl, "Would you like to be free from that evil spirit?"

"Yes," she replied. While we were walking out of the room, I took her hands, intending to pray for her.

I said, "In the name of," but before I could get "Jesus" out, she fell to the ground, right in front of the doorway with a full-blown demonic manifestation that looked like a grand mal seizure! I was stunned. The students stood there speechless.

Suddenly I heard the Lord's voice say to me again, "I am going to show off today!"

The pastor looked at me as if to say, "Do something!" I had been involved in many deliverances in the past (including my own), but I wasn't sure what was appropriate in this setting.

I leaned over and said, "Leave this woman now in Jesus' name!" Instantly she was delivered. (Those university demons are smarter than the ones I had dealt with previously.) She began rolling on the floor in a trance-like state, laughing hysterically. It was the kind of laughter that made you laugh.

The pastor said, "We need to get her out of here." We carried her into the hallway. People just stood there watching her as she rolled around and laughed. It was so loud in the hallway that we decided to carry her outside the back door of the university. She continued laughing uncontrollably while she rolled on the ground outside, completely unaware of her environment. More people began to gather. I still wasn't sure what to do, but I noticed that many people, in what was mostly an unsaved crowd, were experiencing manifestations like twitching or electricity running through their bodies. I'd seen this before when the Holy Spirit would touch people powerfully in church settings, but most of these people were not Christians, and this wasn't church!

The next thing I knew, I was pointing to a young man in the crowd and saying, "Do you want some of this?"

"Yes...No...I don't know!" he said.

"Take it!" I said. All at once he fell to the ground, rolling around and laughing. I began to point to others and say the same thing. Within a few moments, several people were on the ground laughing hysterically, while others looked on in amazement.

About 50 yards off in the distance, a young man and woman were standing together holding hands, leaning against a wall. I yelled over to the young man, "Are you a Christian?" He looked shocked.

"No!" he said, as he tried to disappear into the wall.

"Your girlfriend is," I said. "She's been waiting for you to get saved so she can marry you!" She fell to the ground, grabbing him by one leg, crying and screaming.

As I walked toward him I said, "Your parents must be Christians, because I saw your daddy lift you up and dedicate you to the Lord when you were born."

"Yes," he said, "both of my parents are Christians. I am the only one of their five children who is not saved." By now, I was right in front of him. His girlfriend grabbed both of our legs and started praying for his salvation out loud.

I asked him, "What is your name?"

He said, "My name is Joshua."

"Joshua!" I said. "Joshua means Savior! Pray with me," I continued. He received Jesus that day.

The next day, the young man that I had given the word to in class about being a politician ran up to me in the hallway of the university. He said, "Remember what you said to me yesterday about being a politician?"

"Yes," I said.

"Well, I got so nervous that I forgot I was studying political science. I have always wanted to be a politician."

Wow! One of the leaders of witchcraft acknowledged to me that the God of Heaven had a plan for his life.

— FALSE MANIFESTATIONS —

This is just one of the stories I have experienced while using my gifting to right injustice. I have had similar experiences all over the United States. I don't understand people who think that Americans aren't hungry for God. Everywhere I go I see folks who are famished and longing for a spiritual awakening, and we have the ability to demonstrate a gospel of power.

I am convinced that many people who are caught up in witchcraft are the "unpaid bills" of the church. A lot of these folks have experienced spiritual realities and come to our churches to find an explanation for this dimension of life, but only find a powerless religion. It is sad but true that most people wouldn't know whether God showed up in church or not, because so little of modern Christianity requires Heaven's intervention. Jesus never expected people to believe in a gospel absent of power. Therefore Jesus said, "If I don't do the works of My Father, do not believe Me" (John 10:37). The people who can't find power in church visit a séance or a cult meeting and find the enemy's counterfeit power. Although it's the dark side, it is real, and they turn to it. If they cannot find supernatural power in the church, they will sadly go to where they can. Proverbs 27:7 says, "To a famished man any bitter thing is sweet."

At Bethel Church, as in many other churches that are rising up in this hour, we see miracles of healing, salvation, and deliverance each week in our services. A while back, a 20-year-old school of ministry student named Lacey was in one of our local bookstores. She observed a young man dressed in black sitting at a table near her. He had long black fingernails and looked pretty scary. To make matters worse he was moving a fork on the table with his mind! Lacey sat down across from him and watched for a while. Then this sweet, beautiful, young lady asked him, "Do you want to see real power?"

"What do you mean by that?" he replied.

"Come to church with me," she said, "and I will show you the power of God." She put him in her Mustang and drove him to church. They arrived a little late and people were already worshiping when they entered the sanctuary. Lacey came up front where I was sitting and said to me in a loud whisper, "Hey Dad, I brought a witch to church. He's in the back, levitating. I told him you would show him the real power of God! Come to the back and pray for him."

"Okay," I replied, "I'll be back there in a few minutes."

A few seconds passed before another parishioner rushed to the front and blurted out, "There's a witch back there! He's levitating!"

"I know," I said. I was told about the young man a couple more times before I finally made my way back to him. I asked him if I could pray for him. Although he seemed reluctant, he said that I could. I put my hands on his shoulders and prayed a simple prayer asking the Holy Spirit to come and show him that God was real. He suddenly slid down the wall and landed on his rear. I joined him on the floor and embraced him. He was stiff as a board. In my mind, the Lord began to show me his life through pictures. I saw the abuse of his mother and father. Then the Lord showed me specific events that had happened in his life. He relaxed and wept quietly.

He had gotten involved in witchcraft to protect himself from his abusive parents. It was clear that the Lord was ministering to some of his deepest wounds. Lacey put him back in her Mustang and took him to his home, which turned out to be under a bridge. On the way home he said to her, "You guys have a psychic in your church."

"No," Lacey responded, "that was the power of God that I told you about."

"That's freaky!" he said. That young man will never be the same after what he experienced that night.

— THE WEAPONS OF OUR WARFARE —

The people in the encounters I've just shared experienced the destruction of the devil's bondage in their lives but the superior power of the Kingdom of God was demonstrated to them. That's what God's justice looks like. The enemy has already been judged, found guilty and sentenced to a powerless existence through the victory of the cross. When we confront his hold on an individual's life, we are only enforcing the decision that has already been made in Heaven.

Notice that while violence was being done to the enemy and his kingdom in these encounters, the people he had been tormenting experienced joy, peace, and healing. And I was merely praying and prophesying. As Christians, we wage most of our "warfare" by doing things that don't look like fighting. We prophesy blessing and destiny over people and cities. We love people sacrificially and bless them when they curse us. We pray for Heaven to come to earth.

God even turns praise and worship into warfare. The Psalmist describes this in Psalm 149:6-8 (NKJV):

> *Let the high praises of God be in their mouth, and a two-edged sword in their hand, to execute vengeance on the nations, and punishments on the peoples; to bind their kings with chains, and their nobles with fetters of iron; to execute on them the written judgment—this honor have all His saints. Praise the Lord!*

Psalm 8:2 (NIV) says, "You have ordained praise because of Your enemies, to silence the foe and the avenger." Our praises silence the enemy, bind him, and execute the written judgment against him.

I pray that all of us discover the power God has put in our hands to bring justice wherever we go. As the apostle Paul promised, "The weapons of our warfare are not carnal but mighty in God for pulling down strongholds" (2 Cor. 10:4 NKJV). When we see the broken and hurting and the need for justice rises up in us, we have all the power that we need in order to act.

Because bringing justice requires us to confront the enemy, we must be people of great courage. As we look at historical accounts of many men and women of courage in the next chapter, we must realize that their courage sets the royal standard. We must embrace our gifting and step forward into the halls of history yet to be written!

Chapter 13

THE DOGS OF DOOM STAND AT THE DOORS OF DESTINY

A coward dies a thousand deaths but a brave man dies only once.

— DYING TO MAKE HISTORY —

IT was a typical hot August evening in Redding, California. Carolyn was dropping by one of the local clothing stores to get a few things before going home. She found a parking space and maneuvered her vehicle into it. Placing the car in park, she shut off the engine. As she reached over to close the passenger side window, a young man in his early twenties came to the driver's side and yelled, "Get out of the car!" It was then that she realized his arm was inside the car and he was holding a gun to her ribs.

Carolyn, who is a rather quiet, modest woman in her mid-fifties said, "Look, you don't want this car. It doesn't run good, hardly has any gas and the air conditioner doesn't work." Then gesturing toward the gun she said, "What's THIS?" "My gun," he said. Feeling the boldness of the Lord rise within her, she looked him straight in the eye and asked, "What are you going to do with it?" Suddenly his whole body relaxed as if he had been holding his breath, "Nothing," he sighed.

"We need to talk," Carolyn said gently. "You've been set up. God wants you to hear what I have to tell you." He nodded, showing her that the gun wasn't even loaded, and putting it back into his pack. The would-be thief knelt by the car while Carolyn began to talk to him, as a mother would talk to her son, about how much the Heavenly Father

155

loved him. He opened up and poured out his heart, sharing his life's troubles and difficulties with her. She asked if he had been contemplating suicide. He told her that he had written a letter to his parents that very morning about wanting to take his life. She ministered to him for nearly an hour. Placing her hand on his bowed head, she prayed for him, and felt an indescribable love pour through her spirit into him. As amazing as it sounds, it was hard for them to say goodbye to one another. They both wanted to remain immersed in God's presence in an encounter neither of them will ever forget.

Disguised as an everyday housewife, Carolyn is a princess who refused to be intimidated by a thug, and instead, radically altered the course of a young man's life!

— LOSING THE FEAR OF DEATH —

People love to hear stories of everyday heroism, but most of us question whether we would have been able to respond so boldly. There are plenty of other stories where people see evil, yet do nothing, caring more to save their own lives rather than living sacrificially.

This survival mentality has no place in the hearts and minds of the sons and daughters of the King. Jesus said, "For whoever wishes to save his life will lose it; but whoever loses his life for My sake will find it" (Matt. 16:25). The survival mentality is a finite core value that restricts the impact of our lives to the here-and-now and robs us of the history-making exploits that have been assigned to each of us by God Himself.

Our survival mentality is supposed to be dealt with at baptism. Jesus said, "If anyone wishes to come after Me, he must deny himself, and take up his cross and follow Me" (Matt. 16:24). Resurrection life lies on the other side of the crucifixion. To be disciples of Christ we must deal with death head-on. We do this by taking up our cross and following Jesus to the crucifixion at the baptismal tank.

Or do you not know that all of us who have been baptized into Christ Jesus have been baptized into His death? Therefore we have been buried with Him through baptism into death, so that as Christ was raised from the dead through the glory of the Father, so we too might walk in newness of life. For if we have become united with Him in the likeness of His death, certainly we shall also be in the likeness of His resurrection (Romans 6:3-5).

When we carry our cross down to the baptismal tank, death, which is the last enemy of our soul, is destroyed and we begin to experience resurrection life. The writer of Hebrews said it best:

Therefore, since the children share in flesh and blood, He Himself [Jesus] likewise also partook of the same, that through death He might render powerless him who had the power of death, that is, the devil, and might free those who through fear of death were subject to slavery all their lives (Hebrews 2:14-15).

Just imagine what a whole army of living "dead" people can accomplish when they are no longer intimidated by the grave, but are filled with the boldness of God! Royal people live from eternity and therefore don't view physical death as an end, but as an entrance to a new dimension in God.

When we meet a believer who loves the gift of life yet has no fear of death, we've met a person who is free to really live. I saw this first-hand in my friend, Bob Perry. In 2000 I got pretty sick. There was a chance that I had a serious life-threatening illness, and it paralyzed me with the fear of death. One day I called Bob, who had survived kidney cancer several years before after being told by the doctors that he wasn't expected to live.

I asked him, "Were you ever afraid to die?"

"No!" he said.

"Why not?" I asked.

"You can't threaten me with Heaven!" he proclaimed.

— Defying Death —

I am convinced that true courage is only born in those who have dealt with the fear of death. There are a lot of imitators—people who look brave on the outside but are scared little children on the inside. Some of the toughest-looking people in the world are really rocked by fear. People who have dealt with death are dangerous. You can't stop them because there is nothing else to threaten them with.

Jason McNutt was a Bethel School of Supernatural Ministry student who personified this. Jason went to Peru to minister on the streets and a man came up to him and pulled out a gun. He pointed it at his head and said, "Shut up! Stop preaching or I am going to kill you!" Jason looked him right in the eye and responded, "Go ahead, shoot me. I came here to die!" The man ran away!

— Refuse to Be Intimidated by the Elements —

Another student, Bobby Brown, refused to be intimidated by the elements (the powers of this world) and instead grabbed his moment to be remembered in history. He went on a School of Ministry trip to Tijuana, Mexico, with about 60 other students. The police chief of that city had met the Lord not long before and gave our team a permit to preach in the downtown square on Revolution Street. Right after our students got the sound equipment set up, rain began to pour down. The ministry students gathered in a circle to pray about what to do. Bobby suddenly felt God tell him to go to the microphone and make an announcement. He jumped up on the stage and proclaimed, "Jesus loves you! He is going to prove it right now by stopping the rain."

He pointed to the clouds and shouted, "Rain, stop now! Clouds, roll back!" In one second the rain stopped and the clouds rolled back. The people were stunned! A lady in the third story of an apartment building across the street yelled out in Spanish, "I want to receive this Jesus!" Bobby led her to Christ over the P.A. system. She raised her hands to heaven to thank God. Just then the power of the Lord came through her window and knocked her to the floor!

— COURAGE IN THE MARKET PLACE —

My favorite story to date is that of Chad Dedmon. Chad is a newly-wed who recently graduated from BSSM. A few months ago he went into a local supermarket to buy some doughnuts. While he stood in line to pay for his food, he noticed that the woman in front of him was wearing hearing aids. Chad asked her a few questions and found out that she was completely deaf in one ear and 50 percent deaf in the other. He asked if he could pray for her and, with her permission, put his hands on her ears and commanded them to be healed. He then convinced her to take out her hearing aids. She discovered that she was completely healed and could hear perfectly. The lady was crying, and so was the cashier who was observing the whole thing.

Chad asked the cashier if he could get on the loudspeaker and ask other people in the store if he could pray for them, because God had shown him more healings that He wanted to do for other people. The lady agreed and handed him the microphone.

"Attention all shoppers! God just healed this deaf lady." He handed the mic to the lady who had gotten healed and asked her to tell the people what God had done. She shared through her tears and then handed the microphone back to Chad.

Chad said, "God has shown me that there is someone here who has a bad left hip and He wants to heal you. Come to aisle 12 and I will pray for you." He announced several other words of knowledge for healing, and within a few minutes people were gathered around the checkstand. A lady drove up in an electric cart and said, "I am the one with the left hip problem. I am getting a hip replacement tomorrow."

Chad prayed for her and then convinced her to test it by walking. This took awhile as the woman refused to get up and walk. She finally did and then started running, yelling, "I am healed, I am healed!"

The encounter ended with two more people getting healed and several people receiving the Lord after Chad preached a message of healing and salvation right there in the store.

Most of us would love to see God move as He did with these students, but if we haven't dealt with our survival mentality, we won't have the strength to step out and grab hold of divine moments of opportunity. When we are afraid, we stay on the porch of our life and we never run with the big dogs! If we take up a defensive posture, we actually yield the position of influence and authority that God has called us to have over the enemy. In the vacuum we leave others who have found a cause worth dying for will rise up with conviction and power from the dark side. Then the great adventure is replaced with a boring and monotonous existence. Fear debilitates us from fighting the good fight that God has called us to. It has been disguised in the Church as "stewardship," "wisdom," and a bunch of other spiritual words, reducing the Christian experience to simply holding the fort. The only convictions that are worth living for are those worth dying for.

Radical Muslims are blowing themselves up in the name of Allah. The world can't figure out why someone would be that crazy. Let me make it clear that I believe these radical Muslims are murderers who take the lives of the innocent. I want no part of their religion. But I recognize the fact that they have something they are willing to die for. Christians should understand what it means to give up their life for a cause, country, covenant, or convictions because we gave up our life when we received Christ. If we don't have the same kind of strong passion and courage to stand up for our convictions, we will forfeit our rightful impact on society to the suicide bombers.

— DYING IN FAITH RATHER THAN LIVING IN DOUBT —

Sometimes courage brings a visible victory, like the stories of our students; other times it doesn't seem like situations end in victory. People in the Kingdom know that they already have the victory, and whether they live or die, their job is to stand on the truth of the gospel.

At Bethel Church, we see many miracles as well as hundreds of people healed every month. We have a staff person who leads a team of people charged with keeping track of testimonies so they can be repeated. Yet sometimes people don't get healed though we've contended for them.

Karen Holt was Bill Johnson's personal assistant when he came to Bethel ten years ago. A year after Bill's arrival she was diagnosed with breast cancer. She refused treatment because she believed that God was going to heal her. Many people were getting healed of the same disease throughout the entire time Karen was sick. Her husband, who was also one of our staff pastors, encouraged her to seek treatment. Many others on the Bethel team counseled Karen to get medical help. She was convinced that Jesus would take care of her. She spent tons of time praying, reading the testimonies of others who got healed of cancer and flying around the country getting the most faith-filled Christians to pray for her. About three years later, she died. We were all stunned. Some said she had wasted her life, but I disagree. Karen chose to die in faith rather than live in doubt. Karen died the way she lived, trusting God. Her life wasn't a waste for those of us who were impacted by her.

— THE LAND OF THE FREE AND THE HOME OF THE BRAVE —

In the last couple of years nearly 2,000 American men and women have died and many more have been wounded in the war in Iraq. It is sad to hear of the scores of lives that are being taken away every day, but the truth is that everybody is going to die someday. The real question that we should ask ourselves is whether or not we are really living. When we leave this world, will our lives actually have counted for something? The greatest tragedy in our world isn't that so many are dying to protect our freedoms, but that millions are living without any purpose!

America is the land of the free and the home of the brave, but what many people have forgotten is that if we were not the home of the brave, we would have never been the land of the free! This motto doesn't describe us as much as it does our forefathers. George Washington's life depicts this Kingdom courage. He was convinced that he could not die until he fulfilled his call in life, which he believed was predestined by his Creator.

There are many stories of George Washington's bravery. The American soldiers he led were ill-prepared and ill-equipped for war. One third of them had no shoes or shirts. They fought with hunting rifles and had little training. George, much like William Wallace in the movie *Braveheart*, would ride back and forth in front of his troops on his huge white horse and exhort his men, yet his troops would often retreat in battle because they were afraid.

In one particular battle, George told his men that he would shoot them in the back if they retreated. They encountered the British and soon, true to nature, the American soldiers turned and ran. George Washington rode right into the worst part of the fray yelling, "If you retreat I will shoot you in the back! Push forward men! Come back or I'll shoot you!" They all ran off, leaving George by himself on the field. Washington was so mad that he rode to the edge of the bluff, which was right in front of the British soldiers, and sat on his horse staring at them. The entire British army unloaded their weapons at him, but miraculously they didn't hit him once. After the shooting, they stood to their feet and applauded him.

In another battle, the British shot two horses out from under Washington. When he returned to camp he had three bullet holes through his coat under both arms, but was untouched. In fact, some historians believe that the British's inability to kill Washington was the main factor in their surrender. A man who wasn't afraid to die caused many others to live in freedom.

— TRUE VICTORY —

In some ways violence is a way of life on this planet. Jesus said "Violent men take the Kingdom by force." (Matt. 11:12) It is evident that we as Christians live in a world that is full of violence, both in the seen and unseen world. It is important for us to understand that our battles are to be the manifestation of His victory. When Jesus died on the cross He won the ultimate triumph. We no longer fight *for* victory but we fight *from* victory. Winning is assured when we enter the battle. The ultimate challenge therefore lies not so much in the battle itself but in getting the people of God to join the fray. When the royal army refuses to fight and instead cowers from combat, they are often shot in the back where they are armor-less. Notice that the "armor of God" in Ephesians has no protection for your back. We are ill-equipped for retreat.

"The dogs of doom stand at the doors of our destiny!" What we believe to be our most fearful stumbling block is actually the door to our greatest victory. Our greatest destiny lies on the other side of fear. Courage is the ability to advance in the face of adversity to obtain these treasures.

— RECOUNTING THE TESTIMONIES OF THE PAST —

One of the challenges in getting Christians to engage in war is their lack of appreciation for the values which moved our forefathers to purchase our freedom with their lives. History helps us connect to virtues worth dying for. They stand behind the veil of time, but are our inheritance. They are often clothed with words like "Honor," "Freedom," "Valor," "Loyalty" and "Respect." Our founding mothers and fathers treated these *invisible attributes* like countries to protect and qualities to pass down to their children. These noble people fought not so much to protect land but to perpetuate the principles of the Kingdom.

When we forget the historic exploits of God, we begin to falter in the absence of true foundations. This often leads us to retreat into self-seeking pleasure as some euphoric goal of life, the result of which is wars being lost before the enemy is ever encountered. Pleasure is seldom found on the battlefield. The Psalmist drove this point home:

> *The sons of Ephraim were archers equipped with bows, yet they turned back in the day of battle. They did not keep the covenant of God*

and refused to walk in His law; they forgot His deeds and His miracles that He had shown them (Psalm 78:9-11).

By recounting testimonies, we honor the past and become cognizant of the ancient boundaries and borders that have been entrusted to our protection. It is through testimonies that we capture the vision of our founding fathers and understand how important it is to pass these testimonies on.

The apostle John wrote, "They overcame him because of the blood of the Lamb and because of the word of their testimony, and they did not love their life even when faced with death" (Rev. 12:11). The elements of victory are recounted to us in this passage. *They overcame him by the blood of the Lamb:* This means we live from His victory instead of trying to get victory. Christians are to be offensively minded. We have the ball. The war has already been won and the only thing that remains is to fight the battles that enforce the victory. The devil has already been defeated. Jesus knocked his teeth out of his mouth. What is he going to do to you, gum you to death?

The word of their testimony: Testimonies remind us of God's repeatable exploits that He has accomplished on the behalf of His people. "The testimony of Jesus is the spirit of prophecy" (Rev. 19:10). In other words, God's miraculous deeds of the past lay the foundation for His glorious acts in our future.

They did not love their lives unto death: There it is again—the power of those who defy death. I am convinced that once the fear of death is broken in our lives, we become an unstoppable force that the hordes of hell cannot contend with. When the devil loses the ability to scare us in death, he becomes powerless in our lives.

— DEALING WITH THE DRAGON LADY —

This revelation was really driven home to me several years ago. We went through a season that I call the "Valley of the Shadow of Death." It all started when a friend of ours named Tracy Evans led a woman they called "The Dragon Lady"(a different Dragon Lady from the one in China) to Christ.

Jane (not her real name) was a woman in her mid-twenties, about six feet tall, with long, stringy brown hair with a blond streak running through it. She was very muscular and hard-looking with deep brown eyes and a weathered face. She had been in Anton LaVey's satanist church in San Francisco for the two years prior to coming to Weaverville. The Dragon Lady, Jane, was known for going into the bars. After having a few drinks she would become like an animal, eat the shot glass and beat up several men in the bar. Everyone in our community feared her.

Tracy was working at our small rural hospital when the police brought Jane in and put her in the "rubber room." She had been slithering on her belly like a snake and hissing like a cat on the pump island of a local service station. Tracy led her to Christ in her padded cell. Later on that night, Tracy came to our house and convinced us to let Jane move in to our home for a while.

Then the drama began! She was scared to death of the dark so she slept on the couch with the lights on. Several times a night she would wake up screaming and yelling at "the demons" that were after her.

I didn't sleep much for weeks. Thankfully, our three small children slept upstairs. I would get up and pray with her and she would fall right back to sleep, but I would stay up for hours with my heart pounding out of my chest.

To make matters worse, other strange things were happening at the same time. People would call us several times a day and tell us that satan was going to kill us, destroy our children and do other disgusting things. The callers knew us by name and it always sounded like there was a séance going on in the background. Often when they would call, the lights would go off in the house and pictures would fall off the walls. The phone would also go dead a couple of times a week while I was talking with them.

My entire family had nightmares most nights and I kept having a large demon with bright red glowing eyes visit me at night. I would wake up with horrible dreams and the dang thing would be standing at the foot of my bed. It would scare the heck out of me! I would break into cold sweats and be completely paralyzed with fear.

This continued for more than six months! We would have kicked Jane out, but she was getting delivered and my family and I were growing in the Lord like crazy. In the midst of all this demonic stuff, there were daily miracles. For instance, one day my daughter, Shannon, cut her finger and it was bleeding all over the place. Jane was holding her hand under the faucet while Kathy got a Band-Aid. Kathy prayed for the finger before she applied the Band-Aid and the cut closed up and healed right in front of their eyes. Jane freaked out! This season in our life was like living in a war-zone where Heaven and hell were violently colliding. Because we persevered through this time, Jane got delivered and became a beautiful woman. Sadly, sometime later on she chose to go back to the world.

As you might imagine, this season taught our family much about warfare and the devil's devious ways. One of the most powerful lessons I learned happened through the "glowing red-eyed demon" experience. It kept intruding into my bedroom at night and nothing I seemed to do would make it leave. I would rebuke it, pray over and anoint my room with oil, read the Bible to the demon, and worship God while it watched but refused to leave. It seemed to be able to sense that I was afraid of it.

Bill Johnson says, "You only have power over the storm that you have peace in." This statement references the story of Jesus sleeping in the boat during a storm. He woke up and calmed the wind by saying, "Peace, be still." (Mark 4:39 NKJV). The Lord spoke to me and told me that I was going to "learn the power of peace." I remembered Paul's words to the Philippians: "You are in no way alarmed by your opponents—which is a sign of destruction for them, but of salvation for you, and that too, from God" (Phil. 1:28). There is just something about courage that causes the enemy to know he is already defeated, because courage is immune to his primary weapon, which is fear. Courage is peace in the storm, the inability to be alarmed by the enemy. When we can sleep in the storm, be calm in the face of battle and not panic in the midst of opposition, we have broken the back of the devil!

The night after this word from the Lord about the power of peace, the demon returned. My heart raced, my head was spinning and I wanted to run or scream. Jesus had already given me a strategy for victory. I looked up from my covers and there it stood. It's huge eyes were glowing red as it stared at me. I looked at it and said, "Oh it's just you!" Then I rolled over and went back to sleep. That was the end of my visitations. From then on I stopped being afraid and started looking forward to the battle. When the demonized people called, I would pick up the phone and share God's love and mercy with them. They didn't know what to do with me after that. They would just hang up. It wasn't long before all the weirdness ceased. Courage manifested through peace is a powerful weapon of warfare. After all, the God of peace is crushing satan under our feet (see Rom. 16:20)!

— THE KINGDOM IS NO PLACE FOR COWARDS —

John wrote, "The cowardly...their part will be in the lake that burns with fire and brimstone, which is the second death" (Rev. 21:8). You can't be a Christian and be a coward! Courage is one of the attributes of royalty that can't be underestimated. Courage is not just seen in the great exploits applauded by men. More often courage lies in the quietness of a life that refuses to bow to the cesspool of darkness that tugs daily at our souls. Here is the kind of courage I see in some of the people I know:

Courage is seen in a young 8-year-old boy who lives in a drug-infested neighborhood. He has never met his father. His mother is a prostitute and a drug addict. His house is filled with violence, dope, sex and the worst filth known to man, but he gets up every Sunday morning, gets himself dressed in his finest clothes, which aren't much to look at, and goes to church. His neighbors make fun of him as he passes by them on his way to church with his little ragged paperback Bible that someone gave him, but he ignores them because he has found a reason to live.

Courage is found in a young lady who ends up pregnant and alone. What began as her first experience of finally being loved, or so she thought, has turned into uncertainty and disillusionment. There is no one to support her. Her boyfriend is gone; her parents are divorced, chasing other lovers, while she finds herself on the streets alone once again. Her future is a mystery and her past is misery, but she chooses to rise above it all. People tell her to abort her child but she welcomes her newborn baby into the world and gives him the love that she never received herself. She is my hero.

Courage can be observed in a mother with three children. Her husband's a manic and raging alcoholic. Violence has become a way of life for them. She has been trying to make the marriage work for years, but he doesn't want a wife; he wants a slave that he can drive with fear, and kids that he can torment into submission. He gives her no money and never allows her or the children to have a life. She has no job skills because she never wants to leave the kids alone in the war zone with their out-of-control father. But one day she decides that it is over. She takes the children and they leave, not knowing where they're going but realizing that they can't stay in this slave camp another day. He has threatened her life many times, but she chooses boldness over fear and life over death. They will start fresh and trust God to lead them.

Courage resides in the young woman who goes to a high school where the number of virgins can be counted on two hands. Everyone around her is "doing it," and she feels the peer pressure and the sex drive within her are trying to defeat her. But she has chosen to save herself for her prince. She realizes that the value of her virginity lies in the struggle that it takes to get it from the battlefield to the honeymoon suite, and she is determined to do it.

History is written by these acts of courage. And not one is better than the other. When we refuse to compromise, we become the people that God can trust to carry His glory to the world.

History will record whether or not we, God's people, rise up with valor in this dispensation to perpetuate the royal attributes of our Holy King, or we digress in fear into the cesspool of moral corruption. If we fail, those who record our history will also be caught in the depth of its despair. If we succeed and rise above the mire of the complacency of our peers, we could very possibly leave a legacy that lasts for eternity. We cannot afford to fail! We must dress ourselves in vigilance and run to protect the virtues that have been handed down to us. With so much at stake we must win the most epic of battles!

Part III:
Introducing the
Authority and Responsibility
of Royalty

IN the previous chapters we have ventured into the courts of the King and observed His royal people. We have learned much about the call, behavior, and values that have caused them to excel beyond all others on the earth.

Jesus said, "To whom much is given from him much will be required (Luke 12:48 NKJV)." Therefore, we must investigate the responsibility that God has given His people, and the authority that coincides with this responsibility to accomplish His mission.

Some may be surprised at the high call of God that rests on us. For many years the church has reduced the call of God down to something that can be accomplished by discipline, wisdom, and the finances of man. This is because we have been uncomfortable with the "mission impossible" message that the Bible clearly articulates. Because of this, the Goliaths of the earth are roaming freely through our cities, stealing, killing, and destroying wherever they go.

The chapters you are about to read are like blasts of a trumpet calling the royal army to take its place on the battlefield. The Son of Man appeared for this purpose—to destroy the works of the devil. We are His battle-scarred hands extended to a wounded and dying people. We have been anointed and equipped to destroy giants and extend the borders of the Kingdom, causing Heaven to collide with earth!

Chapter 14

HIS MAJESTY'S SECRET SERVICE

*Jesus said to make disciples of all the nations,
but the Church has reduced the great commission
down to just making disciples in all nations.*

— ROYAL RESPONSIBILITY AND AUTHORITY —

OUR call to royalty comes with authority and much responsibility. Jesus said, "From everyone who has been given much, much will be required; and to whom they entrusted much, of him they will ask all the more" (Luke 12:48). Authority and responsibility always go together and we must understand both of these aspects of our call. God has invested His church with His authority over everything on earth, but we also have the responsibility to use that authority to fulfill His purposes.

He has commissioned us to disciple the nations. It is important for us to understand our job description so that we can accomplish the will of the Father. Although Jesus said to make disciples *of all nations*, most of the church has reduced our call down to making disciples *in all nations*. So much of the way we read and interpret the Bible has been affected by a pauper mentality. When we feel small and powerless, we tend to dilute the word of God down to something we can accomplish in our own weak state so we don't feel convicted for not doing what's required of us. Therefore, as we begin to be transformed into a royal priesthood, we need to take a fresh look at the Scriptures. Let's start with these verses:

All authority has been given to Me in heaven and on earth. Go there-
fore and make disciples of all the nations, baptizing them in the name of
the Father and the Son and the Holy Spirit, teaching them to observe all
that I commanded you; and lo, I am with you always, even to the end of
the age (Matthew 28:18-20).

There is an obvious difference between discipling people and discipling nations. We know that everyone who comes to Christ needs to be
discipled, as we addressed in the chapter on covenant, but reducing the
Great Commission down to merely discipling people is a complete misunderstanding of the word of God. Notice that Jesus sets discipleship in
the context of *all authority* in Heaven and on earth being transferred
from the devil to Him. *Therefore* (because of this), make disciples of the
nations. In order for us to really comprehend the Great Commission, we
have to understand the history of the earth and how God intended to
govern the world. Let's venture back to the Book of Genesis and see
how the earth was intended to be ruled.

In the beginning of creation Adam and Eve were given authority to
rule the earth. Look at this passage in the Book of Genesis:

Then God said, "Let Us make man in Our image, according to Our
likeness; and let them rule over the fish of the sea and over the birds of
the sky and over the cattle and over all the earth, and over every creeping
thing that creeps on the earth." God created man in His own image, in
the image of God He created him; male and female He created them. God
blessed them; and God said to them, "Be fruitful and multiply, and fill the
earth, and subdue it; and rule over the fish of the sea and over the birds
of the sky and over every living thing that moves on the earth" (Genesis
1:26-28).

We can only imagine what our world would be like if Adam and Eve
had fulfilled their commission to rule. At some point, the devil came to
them in the form of a serpent and convinced them to listen to him
rather than God. When they obeyed the devil they became his slaves
and were forced to surrender their place of authority to him. Since the

fall, satan, "the god of this world," has ruled the earth. His words to Jesus in the wilderness show us that he possessed the realms of dominion that were formerly man's: "The devil said to Him [Jesus], 'I will give You all this domain and its glory; *for it has been handed over to me*, and I give it to whomever I wish'" (Luke 4:6).

Satan ruled man and controlled the nations. When Jesus died on the cross, He stripped the keys of authority away from the devil (see Col. 2:15; Rev. 1:18). He restored His rulership back to mankind and delegated His authority to the Church. That's why the Great Commission begins with the statement, "All authority has been given to me in heaven and *on earth*." Jesus is highlighting the fact that satan no longer has authority in Heaven or on the earth.

In the Book of Ephesians, Paul gears his teaching toward helping us comprehend this incredible reality. The call of God on the saints is so stunning that Paul has to stop in the middle of his letter and pray for us to be enlightened so that we can grasp it.

He writes:

> *I pray that the eyes of your heart may be enlightened, so that you will know what is the hope of His calling, what are the riches of the glory of His inheritance in the saints, and what is the surpassing greatness of His power toward us who believe. These are in accordance with the working of the strength of His might which He brought about in Christ, when He raised Him from the dead and seated Him at His right hand in the heavenly places, far above all rule and authority and power and dominion, and every name that is named, not only in this age but also in the one to come. And He put all things in subjection under His feet, and gave Him as head over all things to the church, which is His body, the fullness of Him who fills all in all* (Ephesians 1:18-23).

Let's read this again: "He gave Him as head over all things to the church!" What an incredible statement. No wonder Paul prayed for us before he shared this with us. The church is the fullness of Christ on the earth. We are to demonstrate His dominion over all powers, empowered by the same Spirit who raised Christ from death. This passage explicates how the primary elements of authority, power and jurisdiction, have been given to the Church. We have jurisdiction by being in relationship with Christ who is seated "far above all rule and authority," and we have the power of "the strength of His might which he brought about in Christ when He raised Him from the dead." How can we help but have all we need to fulfill the Great Commission?

— BORN TO RULE THE WORLDS —

The restoration of authority to mankind through Christ was prophesied in the Book of Daniel. Daniel had a powerful vision that rocked him, and much of it has been misunderstood for years. Although the vision has several parts, I want to take the portion of the vision that is clearly dated. I will show you what I mean by this as you read on. Here are the verses:

> *I kept looking in the night visions, and behold, with the clouds of heaven One like a Son of Man was coming, and He came up to the Ancient of Days and was presented before Him. And to Him was given dominion, glory and a kingdom, that all the peoples, nations and men of every language Might serve Him. His dominion is an everlasting dominion which will not pass away; and His kingdom is one which will not be destroyed* (Daniel 7:13,14).

After Daniel received this part of the vision an angel came to him and gave him the interpretation:

> *As for me, Daniel, my spirit was distressed within me, and the visions in my mind kept alarming me. I approached one of those who were standing by and began asking him the exact meaning of all this. So he told me and made known to me the interpretation of these things...* "*But the saints of the Highest One will receive the kingdom and possess the kingdom forever, for all ages to come*" (Daniel 7:15-16,18).

It would be good to read the entire chapter to get a feel for the context of these Scriptures, but I want to draw attention to one particular detail. The "Son of man" in Daniel's vision is specifically interpreted by the angel as the *saints*. In the vision, the Son of man received "dominion, glory and a kingdom," and in the interpretation, the saints received "the kingdom." This is so dramatic—it is the *saints* who are receiving dominion, glory, and an everlasting Kingdom!

The question is: *when* is dominion, glory, and a kingdom given to the saints? Let's read on:

> *I kept looking, and that horn was waging war with the saints and overpowering them until the Ancient of Days came and judgment was passed in favor of the saints of the Highest One, and the time arrived when the saints took possession of the kingdom* (Daniel 7:21-22).

The timing is very specific here. The two things that mark the timeline for the saints to rule are *judgment being passed in the courts of Heaven in favor of the saints and the saints receiving a kingdom.*

Paul speaks about this court case in the Book of Colossians. Here he tells us that when Jesus died on the Cross something happened in the courts of Heaven. Decrees that had been spoken against us were destroyed, certificates of debt were canceled, and rulers and authorities were disarmed. This is the same court case that Daniel saw many years before. Paul specifically uses judicial terms that confirm "the court sat for judgment" and we received a favorable settlement when Jesus died on the Cross for our sins.

Here is the proclamation from Heaven's court:

> *Having been buried with Him in baptism, in which you were also raised up with Him through faith in the working of God, who raised Him from the dead. When you were dead in your transgressions and the uncircumcision of your flesh, He made you alive together with Him, having forgiven us all our transgressions, having canceled out the certificate of debt consisting of decrees against us, which was hostile to us; and He has taken it out of the way, having nailed it to the cross. When*

He had disarmed the rulers and authorities, He made a public display of them, having triumphed over them through Him (Colossians 2:12-15).

The second sign of the times was that the saints would receive a kingdom. Therefore, it is important to know when do (or when did) the saints receive a kingdom? The following Scriptures give us insight into this mystery: in Matthew 10:7, Jesus preached the Kingdom everywhere he went. He said, "The kingdom of heaven is at hand." He taught us that the born-again experience caused us to, "see the kingdom" (John 3:3); that in order to enter the Kingdom, we must become child-like (Mark 10:15); and He exhorted us to not worry about what to eat, where to live or what to wear, but in all things, seek the Kingdom first and He would provide (see Matt. 6:27-34).

Jesus also preached to the people of His day saying, "There are some of those who are standing here who will not taste death until they see the Son of Man coming in His kingdom" (Matt. 16:28). Then He sent the disciples out to, "Proclaim the kingdom of God and to perform healing" (Luke 9:2). Most importantly, He directly told us that He has given us the Kingdom: "Do not be afraid, little flock, for your Father has chosen gladly to give you the kingdom" (Luke 12:32).

By now the point should be very obvious to us. When we received Jesus as Lord and Savior, we were given the Kingdom! This reality is described throughout the Scriptures. The word "kingdom" is used more than 150 times in the New Testament alone. The apostles also carried on the Kingdom proclamation throughout the Book of Acts and the Epistles. We can't get away from it—the saints have received a Kingdom, in fulfillment of what Daniel saw in a vision a long time ago.

Wow! If judgment has already been passed in favor of the saints and we received the Kingdom, then we should look at the rest of what Daniel had to say about the day we live in:

He (the servant of the devil) will speak out against the Most High and wear down the saints of the Highest One, and he will intend to make alterations in times and in law; and they will be given into his hand for a time, times, and half a time. But the court will sit for judgment, and his dominion will be taken away, annihilated and destroyed forever. Then the sovereignty, the dominion and the greatness of all the kingdoms under the whole heaven will be given to the people of the saints of the Highest One; His kingdom will be an everlasting kingdom, and all the dominions will serve and obey Him (Daniel 7:25-27).

The saints were born to rule and reign with Christ now! Paul declared that "those who receive abundance of grace and of the gift of righteousness will *reign in life* through the One, Jesus Christ" (Rom. 5:17 NKJV). Of course, we must also understand that God's idea of reigning is much different than the world's. Jesus made it plain that His leaders govern in an empowering way that draws out the best in people.

— TRAINING NATIONS FOR PEACE —

The prophet Isaiah looked into the future and saw the reign of the Body of Christ in the last days. Here is what he envisioned:

Now it will come about that in the last days the mountain of the house of the Lord will be established as the chief of the mountains, and will be raised above the hills; and all the nations will stream to it. And many peoples will come and say, "Come, let us go up to the mountain of the Lord, to the house of the God of Jacob; that He may teach us concerning His ways and that we may walk in His paths." For instruction will go forth from Zion and the word of the Lord from Jerusalem. And He will judge between the nations, and will render decisions for many peoples; and they will hammer their swords into plowshares and their spears into pruning hooks. Nation will not lift up sword against nation, and never again will they learn war (Isaiah 2:2-4).

Mountains are the prophet's metaphor for "authorities," and "the house of the Lord" is the Church. Isaiah is saying that in the last days the Church will be the chief authority on how to live life and make decisions. This will result in the nations coming to us and learning God's ways, much like the Queen of Sheba did in Solomon's day. Weapon plants will be converted into grain silos, automobile manufacturing plants, and other beneficial resources, because the nations won't be fighting with each other any more.

— THE EARTH WAS GIVEN TO THE SONS OF MEN —

The fact that the Church has been restored to man's original position of dominion on earth requires us to learn and carry out the responsibilities that come with our authority. What is the purpose of our dominion? We are called to fulfill the original commission given to Adam and Eve, but the task is different because we must not just subdue the earth but restore it from centuries of destruction it has suffered under the devil's tyranny. The Church is called to destroy every work of the devil, as Jesus modeled, to make disciples of the nations, and to teach the world to obey the commands of Christ.

Those in the church who still think like paupers feel powerless, and so they often distance themselves from the challenges and troubles of the world, sometimes without even knowing they're doing it. They commonly develop doctrines that release them from any responsibility for things that are wrong or evil. One of the biggest problems I have with people interpreting disasters as God's judgment or declaring that, "the kingdom is also 'not yet,' so we just need to ride it out until the millennium," is that those perspectives leave people in a place where they can't and shouldn't do anything about the world around them. As we can see from our study of the Word, God has called us to be His answer to the world's troubles, not to run from them.

People often ask, "If God is so good then why does He let so many bad things happen in the world?" The question isn't, why does God allow bad stuff to happen; the question is, why do saints of the Most High allow them to happen? The Psalmist wrote, "The heavens are the heavens of the Lord, but the earth He has given to the sons of men" (Ps. 115:16). The saints have been given responsibility for the earth! We need to understand this.

Jesus reinforced this idea when He taught us to pray. Let's put on our royal glasses and read the Lord's Prayer.

> *Our Father who is in heaven, Hallowed be Your name. Your kingdom come. Your will be done, on earth as it is in heaven. Give us this day our daily bread. And forgive us our debts, as we also have forgiven our debtors. And do not lead us into temptation, but deliver us from evil. For Yours is the kingdom and the power and the glory forever. Amen* (Matthew 6:9-13).

We can learn several things from these verses. The first thing we see is that the Lord desires to have His will done on earth in the same way that it is done in Heaven. That is a huge revelation. We are to pray and believe God that earth would be modeled after Heaven, as Bill Johnson explains in his book *When Heaven Invades Earth*.

We also receive insight for *how* the earth can be impacted by Heaven. One of the key words that Jesus uses in His model prayer is the word "our." What does "our" mean to us? Let me give an example of what I am trying to say.

Not long ago I was preaching in our church on a Sunday morning. During my message I held up a newspaper article that was written that week about our city. The article was filled with bad news. I said to our congregation, "Did you notice in the Lord's prayer that Jesus had us pray 'Our Father,' and not 'My Father?' Do you remember that He taught us to pray that earth would be like Heaven? How does earth become like Heaven?" I held up the article again and said, "How large is 'our'? Is it 'me and my three', or does 'our' encompass our entire city?"

I continued reading some more of the content of the article, which was filled with alarming statistics. Our divorce rate was one of the highest in the country, violent crime was growing and terminal illnesses were beginning to soar.

Then I said, "Is this our problem, or is the fact that it isn't our problem the real problem? *Whatever I own, I will take responsibility for.* Do you read this article and say to yourself, 'Those poor people,' or are you moved to prayer and called to action when you are informed about our problems?" Then I shouted, "This has to matter to us if we are going to see our city invaded by Heaven!"

When people come to me to tell me about something that needs to change in the church and begin their exhortation by saying, "The church needs," or "Your church needs," I know they are not going to be a part of the solution. They have already distanced themselves from the problem in their hearts by using the words "The church" or "Your church." When they ask, "Do you know what *our* church needs?" I know that they are ready to be a part of the solution.

Unfortunately much of the abdication of responsibility on the part of the Church is the result of cultural influence. American culture has promoted a self-serving individualism to the point where community life is under attack on all fronts. Most people have very little awareness how their choices affect the community around them. If we are going to wake up and take ownership of our communities, we will by necessity confront the individualism around us and in us. One way to get a glimpse of our true attitude regarding our responsibility is to ask ourselves if we treat every person we meet like family. Jesus taught us to pray with a corporate prayer addressed to "Our Father," which reveals God's desire for His people to identify with the situations of their neighbors and community as if they were all in the family of God.

— TRANSFORMING CITIES —

We must let a sense of ownership permeate the way we think about the land and community around us. When we begin to identify ourselves with the future of our cities, we will start praying prayers that will shift the spiritual atmosphere and bring the kingdom of Heaven.

In the early '90s, my family and I started feeling a strong burden for Lewiston, a small town in the mountains of northern California about a half hour from our house. Although this was a community of less than a thousand people, crime, drugs, and immorality were running rampant there. It was the worst town in Trinity County. The Sheriff's Department was perplexed with how to solve the problem and the older residents were up in arms because criminal activities were growing.

The Lord began to talk to us about becoming the answer for this community. We didn't really know what to do. The problem seemed huge, and frankly, we were scared of the violent people who were at the heart of the real issues.

We began to walk the town every week praying over houses. The Lord would often tell us what was going on inside certain homes and show us where the strongholds were. We would stand outside those homes and quietly pray for them. Many times we would get prophetic words that would be the answer to the troubles that we could see in the Spirit. We would prophesy that life would come to those "dead bones" in those homes.

We prayed over the city weekly for a year. We prayed after dark so that we would not be conspicuous and stand out as religious freaks. We weren't doing this to be noticed by man but to be recognized by hell and to be honored by Heaven. We felt such a burden for these people that it caused us to pray many times in the rain and snow. We never missed a week for a solid year. We were determined to see the kingdom of God destroy the works of the devil in Lewiston.

At the end of the long year of warfare, on a moonless and cold winter night, about fifteen people joined us to walk through the community and pray over the city. We split up in teams of two and prayer-walked the Lewiston subdivision for a couple of hours. Later, we met in the gravel parking lot of an old abandoned gym. The gym lay in front of a large field overgrown with weeds. We held hands and began to pray for the people of the community. Within seconds an incredibly loud, blood-curdling voice started screaming from the midst of the field. It sounded like the deep voice of a man writhing in pain. It made our skin crawl. The voice echoed through the valley on that dark, eerie night. When we would stop praying the voice would stop but as soon as we would begin praying the screaming would start again. We decided to pray more fervently until it quit for good. A long while passed as we battled that evil spirit over the town and finally the voice lost strength, got very faint and went silent. It was a strange experience, but we knew that we had received a breakthrough that night.

Within a week the Trinity County Probation Department called and asked if we would like to work with them in Lewiston. They had about 35 teenagers on probation and they were going to teach their parents twice a week for a month. They wanted us to minister to the kids while they were doing parental training with their folks.

We were scared but excited to work with teenagers in Lewiston. The community gave us the abandoned gym to use for free. It was a mess, not having been used for years. It leaked when it rained and it was freezing cold in the winter. We cleaned it up the best we could. The first several months were wild. I broke up four fistfights the first night, wrestling guys to the floor to get them to stop killing each other. We would play basketball and volleyball for an hour and then take a break. During half-time I would share a relevant message with them concerning the things they were going through. Most of my messages gave them tools to deal with life and let them know how valuable they were to God.

They weren't required to stay in the gym for the message, although most of them did. Little by little we became a big family. We met twice a week over the next five years and loved on those kids. The group grew to more than one hundred. Several drug pushers joined us most nights. We made rules about not selling drugs in or around the gym. It was also against the rules to bring weapons into the gym. After a year or so, they began to have a lot of respect for us and they would keep the rules and even police themselves. If someone new came to the gym and tried to sell drugs, the older kids would go over and let them know that the gym was off-limits for drug trafficking.

The Sheriff Deputies messed up our youth group for a while because they would come into the gym and arrest our kids who had warrants. I finally convinced them to arrest them somewhere else and to let us minister to them first.

The community was so touched by what we were doing that they gave us two awards. The Lions Club paid for all the refreshments. Everyone in the county knew what we were doing and were very supportive. That is, of course, except for the religious people. They thought that we should "Bible-bang" the kids and talk to them about their cussing and other obvious outward problems. We were more concerned about their hearts.

Over the next five years the entire town changed. Drug-dealers got saved and most of the kids began respecting themselves and started having moral standards. We taught the teenagers how to deal with conflict so that the fighting stopped and the entire community cleaned up.

If you drive through Lewiston now, you will see a beautiful mountain town nestled in the Trinity Alps. The homes are nice, the yards are well taken care of, the gym is remodeled and there is a great ball park where the overgrown field once was.

There is so much more to this story that it would take the entire book to tell you about it, yet what I learned firsthand through that experience is that we in the Body of Christ have what it takes to see our cities transformed. If we are willing to follow the burden in our hearts and take ownership for our community beyond what is expected, God will give us the strategies and strength to see breakthrough happen.

The Body of Christ is equipped to bring the kingdom of righteousness, peace and joy wherever we go. We have power over the evil prince who keeps people in bondage. We have love that causes people to know they are cared about. We have grace that gives them the power to change. We have mercy that picks them up when they fall. We have courage that stands in the face of violence and brings peace, and we have wisdom that shows people how to live. Most of all, we have an awesome Father who knows how to melt the hearts of His people. We have the answers to the world's problems and the devil's devices.

John said, "The Son of God appeared for this purpose, to destroy the works of the devil" (1 John 3:8), and a few verses later he declared, "As He is, so are we in this world" (4:17b KJV). Let us not stop short of imitating every work of Jesus Himself, for He has all authority in Heaven and on earth and has commissioned us to represent Him in His fullness. He was the One who promised we, His royal family, would do even "greater works than these" (John 14:12).

Chapter 15

PASSING THE BATON

(BY BILL JOHNSON)

A righteous man leaves an inheritance to his children's children
(Proverbs 13:22).

ROYAL families take a great deal of effort to preserve and pass on their family history. Each individual in a generation of royalty only understands his identity by locating himself at the end of a line of ancestors who have all achieved various accomplishments during their reign. It is only in the context of this history that kings and queens will be able to plan and make decisions during their own lifetimes which will continue the royal legacy.

As believers we have been grafted into the rich history of God's royal priesthood, and understanding that history from God's perspective is an essential ingredient in defining what our royal responsibilities are. The Bible is God's history book. It reveals not only His acts and interventions in human history, but what they mean. When studied by those who have truly come to know Him, it reveals a clear plan from beginning to end to establish God's Kingdom. In Genesis, God commissioned Adam and Eve in the Garden of Eden, to be fruitful, multiply, and subdue the earth. In other words, they were to extend the borders of the garden, which expressed the *nature* of God's Kingdom through fruitfulness and multiplication generation after generation.

The nature of the Kingdom of God is that it is always increasing. Isaiah 9:7 says, "There will be no end to the increase of His government or of peace." The Kingdom is always meant to advance in us individually and corporately as the Lord takes us "precept upon precept; line upon line" (Isa. 28:13 KJV), "from glory to glory" (2 Cor. 3:18), and "from faith to faith" (Rom. 1:17).

Given the nature of the Kingdom and God's original commission to Adam and Eve, it is clear that God intended His Kingdom to advance with each succeeding generation. Because each generation would increase in number as they "multiplied," there would be more people to enforce the rule and reign of God on the earth. The Kingdom increases as His people increase, because "in a multitude of people is a king's glory" (Prov. 14:28).

— INHERITANCE —

The key ingredient in this process of increase is inheritance. Inheritance is the link between the generations. It is what each generation receives from the previous generation, and then what they pass on to the next. When one generation has been "fruitful and multiplied," the next generation starts out ahead of where they would have had to start in a certain area of life. For example, a financial inheritance will enable a young couple to buy a house or a car much earlier than they could if they had to depend solely on their own incomes.

If, as God's royal priesthood, we understand that it is by inheritance that God wishes to establish each generation to advance His Kingdom, we must recognize what that makes us responsible for. When we receive an inheritance, we are freely getting what someone else paid a price for. Inheritance makes each generation responsible to both receive and honor what has passed on from the previous generation, and then pay their own price to make it grow so that the next generation starts ahead of them. The ceiling of one generation must become the floor of the next. In our lifetime, this requires us to act with an awareness that our actions affect generations ahead of us. This is precisely the effect that righteousness will have on the way we think, because "a righteous man leaves an inheritance to his children's children."

— REVELATION —

But what constitutes the inheritance of the Kingdom? What do we receive from our royal history, and what are we to give to those ahead of us? After God established His covenant with the people of Israel at Mount Sinai, Moses made this statement: "The secret things belong to the Lord our God, but those things which are revealed belong to us and to our children forever, that we may do all the words of this law" (Deut. 29:29 NKJV). "Revelation," or the "things which are revealed," is the inheritance of the Kingdom.

The importance of revelation from God's perspective is so great that the Bible says we perish without it (see Hos. 4:6). Revelation does not come to make us smarter or give us better doctrinal statements. Revelation is first intended to launch us into divine encounters, where the nature of God is understood and demonstrated through human experience. If revelation does not lead us to a divine encounter, it only works to make us more religious and arrogant, because the nature of knowledge is that it puffs up (see 1 Cor. 8:1). If we have knowledge without an encounter, our pride can actually prohibit us from encountering God. Those who knew the most about God in Jesus' day failed to recognize His Son as He spoke and worked miracles in front of them. Jesus rebuked the Pharisees for this in John 5:39-40 (NKJV): "You search the Scriptures, for in them you think you have eternal life; and these are they which testify of Me. But you are not willing to come to Me that you may have life."

— PERSONAL TRANSFORMATION —

Revelation that does lead us to divine encounter will bring breakthrough that causes a personal transformation. Revelation is the key to spiritual growth because it takes us where we cannot go ourselves. We experience "encounters" because we need "signs" in order to get to where we haven't gone before. I don't need signs when I travel familiar roads, but I have to have signs if I'm going to travel where I've never been.

The second thing revelation does is that it enlarges the playing field of our faith. Hebrews 11:1 says, "Now faith is the substance of things hoped for, the evidence of things not seen." Practically, faith is our understanding of the nature of the invisible realm and how we expect it to influence the visible realm. If our understanding of the nature of God includes the belief that one of the "mysterious ways" He works is to make people sick in order to humble them, we will not expect Him to heal them. But when we have a revelation of the nature of God as the "Sun of Righteousness," who arises "with healing in His wings," (Mal. 4:2) and we see that Jesus healed every person who came to Him without exception, our faith will operate in a larger space. A person with the first belief probably doesn't pray for the sick, or if they do, they pray for perseverance. A person with revelation takes authority over the sickness and commands the sick person's body to be healed "on earth as it is in heaven."

If revelation is meant to be the inheritance of the Kingdom, it is clear that God intends for more than information to be passed on to the next generation. The fruit of revelation is personal transformation and supernatural demonstrations of the nature of God. Therefore, the inheritance of revelation is the inheritance of models, heroes who *became* a revelation of God's nature, and the testimonies of their teaching and exploits.

— TESTIMONY IS THE SPIRIT OF PROPHECY —

So how does one receive this sort of inheritance, use it, and work to multiply it for the next generation? We've already mentioned the study of history, and God felt this was so important that He built in times of remembrance to Israel's calendar. Each of their feasts or fasts revolves around remembering the acts and laws of God. Because of the nature of testimony, remembering the past was meant to ignite a passion in the hearts of each generation to know the God of their fathers in their own day.

The root of the word "testimony" is a word that means, "do again." Every time we repeat the stories of God's invasions into human history, we are calling Him to reveal Himself as the same God today. For this reason, we cannot truly receive our spiritual inheritance if we mean only to applaud the accomplishments of our ancestors. We do not honor the memory of God's heroes by just remembering them. We only honor them if we imitate them by coming to know the God they knew and calling Him to bring His Kingdom in our day.

— THE TRAGEDY OF REVIVAL —

If we study the Old Testament we notice that every time the Israelites failed to keep the Book of the Law in their mouths and remember their history in God, they fell away from Him. As a result, the revealed things that were meant to belong to their children's children forever, though not lost, were forgotten. Each succeeding generation was unaware of their inheritance. If we have an inheritance we don't know about, we won't be able use it.

Sadly, the history of Christian revival is so much like the history of Israel. History shows that revivals typically last two to four years. Many have concluded that this pattern indicates that revivals are only meant to last long enough to give the Church a shot in the arm. But as we have seen, the nature of the Kingdom is advancement and increase. God never intended for His people to live for any season without the outpouring of His Spirit. That outpouring was always meant to increase from the Day of Pentecost until the day Jesus returns.

The increase of God's Kingdom in revival is typified in the Old Testament by Israel's conquest of the Promised Land. When they crossed the Jordan River, God told the people that the land was theirs. However, it was still enemy-occupied, on purpose. If God had driven the enemies out, wild beasts would have taken over the land. So they invaded by degrees, taking a city by a heavenly strategy, occupying the land, and then advancing to the next region until the borders were established. In revival, realms where the kingdom of darkness has been ruling are overcome by the Kingdom of God. The work of the enemy who kills, steals, and destroys is undone as people experience the work of the cross in healing, salvation, and deliverance. The fruit of revival is the Kingdom of God being expressed in every area of society.

Revival always comes through revivalists, men and women of God who become so gripped by a passion for God's Kingdom and so surrendered to the King that He commissions them with authority and power to bring the Kingdom through prophetic revelation and signs and wonders. They are pioneers and trailblazers, bushwhacking their way into enemy territory and claiming it for the Kingdom. They are given spikes in human experience that can be clearly recognized as the fruit of a supernatural anointing.

For example, John Wesley broke into a realm of anointing in preaching the Word that was so powerful that he could be heard over crowds of thousands. The power of God would fall so strongly as he preached that they would commonly warn people to avoid climbing into trees to hear him speak. Inevitably people would ignore the warning, and the crowd would later hear the thuds of people falling out of trees under the power.

Maria Woodworth-Etter drew the attention of newspapers in the late 1800s as many people in her meetings fell into trances and saw visions of Heaven and hell. She also heard reports of people who would fall under the power of God up to a hundred miles away from her meetings. John G. Lake had so many healings in his ministry in Spokane, Washington, that at one point, it was declared the healthiest city in the United States.

But so many of the movements that began with these great men and women, far from seeing an increase in power and anointing, have only seen decline. There are probably a couple of reasons for this. One is that, while the children of revival may have recognized and applauded the miracles of God which their fathers demonstrated, they were unwilling to endure the ridicule and persecution their fathers faced. Another reason is that they failed to understand the principle of inheritance and the nature of the Kingdom. As a result, they built monuments to the past instead of realizing they had a responsibility to take it to the next level for the following generation.

— UNOCCUPIED REALMS —

When the Israelites stopped occupying and advancing into the Promised Land, their enemies started encroaching on their borders. When the realms of God that have been broken into in revival fail to be occupied and advanced by the next generation, the same things happen. Luke 11:24-26 (NKJV) describes this principle:

> *When an unclean spirit goes out of a man, he goes through dry places, seeking rest; and finding none, he says, "I will return to my house from which I came." And when he comes, he finds it swept and put in order. Then he goes and takes with him seven other spirits more wicked than himself, and they enter and dwell there; and the last state of that man is worse than the first.*

Though this principle is being taught here in regard to one person, it is also true of corporate groups and regions. The "house" to which the evil spirit returns can refer to a person, a family, a church, a movement, or a nation. The implication is that, in the Kingdom, the only safe place to be is in the place of occupation and advancement. The moment we work to maintain rather than increase what we've been given is the moment we begin to lose what was given to us. This is what the parable of the talents teaches us. The one who guarded what he was given ended up losing the very thing that was put in his possession. God is not pleased with the posture of maintaining ground.

So much of the church thinks that getting the enemy to leave is the main goal. But if there is a vacuum in the spiritual realm, it will be filled. If we don't fill it with the culture of the Kingdom, it will be reoccupied, and as this verse tells us, the last state will be worse than the first. When the victories of the past generation go unoccupied, they become the platform from which the enemy mocks the victories of the past generation. Worse yet, that unoccupied territory becomes the military encampment from which the enemy launches an assault against the people of God to erase their inherited victories from their memories. For this reason, there are presently regions, cities, families, and ministries once dedicated to the Kingdom that have now become opposing strongholds.

For example, the spiritual descendants of John Wesley and the Holiness movement are now ordaining homosexuals. Once a training center for revivalists, Yale University is now promoting a worldview in complete opposition to the Kingdom. Atlantic City, now a gambling capital, could once count its unsaved citizens on two hands.

It is the failure to occupy and advance the territory won by revivalists that has kept each generation of revival from the benefit of receiving a spiritual inheritance that would allow them to start ahead. Each generation of revival is spiritually fatherless, left to face the multiplied opposition of the enemy in the realms that were once held by the Church. Usually revival comes to the generation that has gotten so sick of enemy intimidation that, like Israel in the days of the Judges, they cry out to God to send a deliverer. And though revival comes, they are not prepared to raise up the next generation to carry it to the next level. A fatherless generation doesn't know how to raise up fathers. The tragedy of revival is that no generation has yet seen the full benefit of spiritual inheritance.

— Exceptions to the Rule —

There are two exceptions to this trend of history that I want to mention in order to catch a glimpse of what can happen when an inheritance is successfully received and passed on. These are by no means the only two. The first is King Solomon. Because his father David won such favor with God, he received a promise that he would always have one of his descendants sitting on his throne. This promise, along with the word that Solomon was to be his heir, led David to train Solomon from birth in the ways of God. Solomon used his inheritance of wisdom to build a kingdom that far exceeded the greatness of his father's. Their two reigns are still known as the Golden Age of Israel.

The second example is Martin Luther. Martin Luther had a revelation that personal faith in Christ was the door to salvation. This teaching caused the biggest church split in history, imposing centuries of enemy occupation in this realm of revelation. In the generations that followed Luther, individuals would sometimes pray for months before truly knowing they were saved. But now, because that revelation has been taught and demonstrated for generations, it is so established that most believers are confident that someone can be sure of their salvation within moments of acknowledging Christ. This expectation has totally changed the way evangelists minister to the lost.

When a realm of God is occupied and advanced in the succeeding generations, part of the Kingdom becomes established as the reality that people will inherit and live in. Unfortunately, so much of the Church has to fight battles that have already been fought in previous generations because, without the successful passing and receiving of inheritance, the revelation was not established. To use the picture in Luke 11, some rooms of the house have been swept out many times, but because they were never furnished, we still cannot live in them. I believe that until the Church has a revelation of God's plan for His Kingdom to be established through inheritance, this cycle of history will repeat itself.

— RECEIVING AND LEAVING OUR INHERITANCE —

Keeping that in mind, I am not saying that the nature of God and His Kingdom have changed. It is still true that His government is increasing, as it is still true that the revealed things belong to His people and the generations to come forever. More than grieved by the past, I am deeply impressed by the opportunity that God has extended to our generation to receive our inheritance and change the course of history by working to raise up a generation of revivalist fathers.

As I mentioned, when "the things which are revealed" are not taught to the next generation, they are not lost, but only forgotten. I believe

that so many mantles (the biblical symbol of God's power and authority) worn by the revivalists of previous generations are not lost, but are
lying where they were left. You can see this in Scripture. Elisha successfully received Elijah's mantle and a double portion of his spirit, but he
died without a successor. And so we have this strange verse in Second
Kings 13:21 (NKJV): "So it was, as they were burying a man, that suddenly they spied a band of raiders; and they put the man in the tomb of
Elisha; and when the man was let down and touched the bones of
Elisha, he revived and stood on his feet." Elisha's miracle anointing was
lying where it was left, still active and intact.

Other realms of anointing and revelation have been buried and
must be unearthed. They are like the wells Jacob had to dig out when
he returned to Canaan. They had been filled with dirt, which is a type of
unredeemed humanity. Moves of God have been halted by men as they
tried to take control or draw glory to themselves, grieving the Holy
Spirit. They block the well of anointing with the dirt of their pride.

The revelations and anointing of our ancestors are in hiding, waiting for us to search them out. It is God Himself who holds them in keeping. As we see in Deuteronomy 29:29, "the secret things belong to the
Lord." However, the radical shift in thinking that Jesus brought was that
God does not hide things *from* us, but *for* us. He said, "It has been given
to [us] to know the mysteries of the kingdom." We have the mysteries
because we have the Holy Spirit. As Jesus promised,

> However when He, the Spirit of Truth, has come, He will guide you
> into all truth; for He will not speak on His own authority, but whatever He
> hears He will speak; and He will tell you things to come. He will glorify Me,
> for He will take of what is Mine and declare it to you (John 16:13-14 NKJV).

Therefore Isaiah's prophecy, "Eye has not seen, nor ear heard, nor
have entered into the heart of man the things which God has prepared
for those who love Him," is amended in First Corinthians 2:10: "But God
has revealed them to us through His Spirit."

God hides things for us because, "It is the glory of God to conceal a matter, but the glory of kings is to search out a matter" (Prov. 25:2). God is glorified by not speaking in plain language to you. He's actually glorified by speaking in parables and symbols and dark sayings. And because the glory of kings is to search out a matter, the royalty that exists in the life of the believer comes to the surface when we realize we have legal access to hidden things and we begin to pursue the unlocking of those mysteries. Those who sit back and say, "Well, whatever God wants me to have I'm happy to receive," are living a pauper's lifestyle in a kingly mansion.

God has given us access to secrets for the realms of politics, business, creativity in the arts, and every other arena of human life. There are realms opening up right now to people because they are realizing they get to search out what God has hidden for them. There are solutions and answers to every problem this world is facing. A failure to comprehend that we have access to mysteries has led the Church to consistently yield her right of authority to contend and pray for transformation.

By surrendering to the notion that everything has to end in tragedy, we fulfill our own prophecies by not stepping into who God has called us to be. We are people who are supposed to be the living answer for the cries and dilemmas of society. It's the royalty in you that will cause you to rise up to say to a problem, "There's an answer for this."

Now those who gain access to realms of revelation and anointing, through rising into their royal call and searching out the matters that have gripped their hearts, will experience a spike in human experience, just as the heroes of history did. But what they and the people of God must realize is that that spike is not to equip just one person to operate in that realm, but to empower that person to equip the Body of Christ to walk in that anointing, in order to establish it as the new norm for Kingdom life.

Bobby Conner says, "God's not interested in somebody; He's interested in His Body." If the Body of Christ will shift into this understanding of the purpose of God's anointing, then leaders will no longer spend their whole life building their ministry, but will focus on raising up the next generation to grow to the next level. And the Body of Christ will learn how to honor and receive from their leaders without falling into the old patterns of either criticizing them or idolizing them so much that they are no longer a standard one must seek to imitate.

— HONORING OUR FATHERS —

We've already seen that honor is one of the essential attributes of men and women in God's royal priesthood. Life is released through honor. But honoring is essentially the proper recognition of those from whom we receive our inheritance. The fifth commandment states, "Honor your father and mother." Honor is the key to receiving our inheritance.

What does honor really look like? Elisha demonstrates honor when he asks for a double portion of Elijah's spirit. Elijah promises that he can have it if Elisha sees him when he's taken up. Simple as that sounds, it turned out to be no easy task. There were sons of the prophets in every town telling Elisha to go home. Elijah himself told him to go home. A chariot of fire from Heaven swooped down between Elisha and Elijah as Elijah was being taken up by a whirlwind. But Elisha didn't blink all day, because he was determined to see Elijah when he was taken. He wouldn't even let him go to the bathroom without him. Then, after the mantle fell, he turned around and parted the river Elijah parted earlier. Elisha's honor was not an accolade or a word of thanks, it was an intense resolve to receive what his spiritual father had to give, and then a boldness to step out and use what he had received.

In the New Testament, Jesus opens the invitation for anyone to receive what Elisha received. He said, "He who receives a prophet in the name of a prophet shall receive a prophet's reward" (Matt. 10:41). As we see with Elisha, receiving the prophet in the name of a prophet means we recognize that we have a requirement to draw on the inheritance he has to give us and use it. The Lord takes it personally when we honor the Christ in someone else. When we honor a prophet in the name of a prophet, we have access to the realm that that person lived in. We may never be called prophets, but something spills over into our lives. There are mantles, realms of God, revelations, and levels of anointing that the individual operated in that we have access to, simply by honoring.

We must embrace our opportunity and responsibility to honor those men and women in history who have broken into different realms of God and advanced the Kingdom, as well as to honor those around us. Honoring those around us doesn't just mean the people with big names. The real challenge is to learn how to know one another after the Spirit so we can recognize the gifts and anointing that God has given to each of the members of His Body. The Lord Jesus, through the apostle Paul, said we're to submit to one another in the fear of Christ. That means we are to honor the Christ in each other.

In fact, Christ and what He purchased for us on the cross are what actually constitute our inheritance. Revelation just tells us what is there, which enables us to use it. Without revelation, the riches of Calvary are like billions of dollars sitting in our bank account that we have no idea about. But even that is a poor comparison, because money can't touch what our inheritance can buy. Ephesians 2 tells us that it's going to take the ages to come just to unfold the richness of His grace. There is so much God has *for* us.

In one week we received reports of two women who were carrying Down's syndrome children in the womb. Different people in our church prayed for them and brought the reports to us that both had been diagnosed differently after they went to the doctors again. They didn't know what happened, but they weren't Down's syndrome children any longer.

We just had another mother come to us in England not too long ago who was pregnant with a child. The doctor told her the baby was dead, and five other consultants all came with the same report: "The baby's not only dead; there's no amniotic fluid. If you don't allow us to remove the child, you will die as well." She came to a conference, received prayer, and she now has a very happy, living child. The ten million dollars in our bank accounts won't fix that one, but the inheritance that we do have, will.

The issue of inheritance is one of the most pressing things on my mind right now. There have been many prophetic words given to the Body of Christ in this season that speak of accelerated growth. I believe that growth will happen as we come into an understanding of inheritance and begin to honor the past generations and each other. Through honor, our inheritance of mantles and realms of revelation and anointing will be released to equip the Body to bring the Kingdom in unprecedented levels and areas. But if we are going to begin receiving our inheritance, we must learn the lesson of history and begin now to position ourselves to leave an inheritance for the next generation. We must also train the next generation to think the same way. We cannot only raise up sons of revival; we must also raise up fathers who will live for generations beyond them.

— OUR FINAL PRIVILEGE —

For me personally, honoring the past includes study of revival history as well as feeding the fire of my own passion to walk in the example of those who have gone before me. I also take any opportunity I can to have descendants of revivalists pray for me. On one occasion I had the privilege of asking John Wimber's young granddaughter to pray for me, and I was overwhelmed by the power and anointing that were released. It confirmed that a person can receive an impartation by honoring someone through honoring their family.

I have the unique experience of being a fifth generation pastor. My kids are the sixth generation. I am so amazed and grateful for my family. But the brand new believer who has no background in God and comes in "honoring the prophet in the name of the prophet" gets in line for the same inheritance we've received. It was never meant to be restricted to those in this highly unusual, favored place. I'm glad I got it, but I have it to give away, not to hoard. I have it to be positioned to take the old norm and raise it up to a new norm. That's life in the Kingdom. If I have access to it, then anyone who comes under the influence of whatever I can give away comes into that inheritance.

My other responsibility is to train my children, both natural and spiritual, to live sacrificially. I give them freely what I have freely received from the Lord, but I tell them, "If you're going to have something to leave to your kids, you'll have to pay a price to develop what you got for free." It's time for the Body of Christ to start thinking and planning and sowing into a generation we will never see. It's time to start constructing a hundred-year vision in our thinking, planning and our prayers. There are so many things I am hungry to see in my day. I've seen so many things I never dreamed I would see, but I've also been impregnated with new dreams, and I cannot be satisfied where I am. I must continually be positioned to occupy and advance. But if I can't see them in my day, I will give all that I have so that my children and my children's children might see them, and so they will have the same heart for the generations.

Do we know why we're surrounded by a cloud of witnesses? In a relay race, the fastest runner on the planet runs the first leg of the race. He can pass the baton to the second fastest runner on the planet, who then passes the baton to the third fastest runner on the planet. But everyone gets a prize according to how the last leg of the race is run. They're all waiting to see what we will do with what we've been given.

We've been given an inheritance of generations. We've been given an inheritance of hundreds of years of mystics, of revivalists, of those who broke into realms of the Spirit to leave something as an inheritance, and it needs to matter to someone. If we take the opportunity we have in this hour to seek out the mysteries hidden for us with a heart to honor those before and beside us, I believe the Church will enter into a day it has never seen. The establishment of the Kingdom of God must increase to such a degree that the normal Christian life truly becomes normal life for everyone in the world.

Chapter 16

BUILDING STRATEGIC ALLIANCES WITH HEAVENLY ALLIES

— AFFECTING THE INVISIBLE REALM —

S PIRITUAL covering is essential for God's royal priesthood to experience the blessing He wants them to have in His family. Though many of us struggle with the issue of submission because of the abuse of authority and the rebellion in our own hearts, it is something we are commanded to do throughout Scripture. The apostle Paul had a lot to say about submitting to leaders, spouses, and one another in the Body. I have to believe he had firsthand experience watching people try to live and minister without the spiritual covering that comes from submission. Acts 19 deliberately contrasts Paul's ministry with exorcists who were trying to minister without a covering.

Now God worked unusual miracles by the hands of Paul, so that even handkerchiefs or aprons were brought from his body to the sick, and the diseases left them and the evil spirits went out of them. Then some of the itinerant Jewish exorcists took it upon themselves to call the name of the Lord Jesus over those who had evil spirits, saying, "We exorcise you by the Jesus whom Paul preaches." Also there were seven sons of Sceva, a Jewish chief priest, who did so. And the evil spirit answered and said, "Jesus I know, and Paul I know; but who are you?" Then the man in whom the evil spirit was leaped on them, overpowered them, and prevailed against them, so that they fled out of the house naked and wounded (Acts 19:11-16 NKJV).

It's amazing that an apostle with a hanky has more power than seven sons of Sceva with the right name. Paul had something they didn't—an apostolic commission. There are two reasons why that is significant: the first is that Paul was an apostle because he was *commissioned* to be one in Acts 13 by the Holy Spirit and by the other church leaders. He was under authority, and Scripture shows us that we only have as much authority as we have submitted to. The centurion in Luke 7 recognized that Jesus had authority because, like him, He was a man "under authority."

The second reason Paul had authority is because he was commissioned as an *apostle*. Although there are other roles and levels of leadership in the church, apostles and prophets are specifically called the foundation of the church (see Eph. 2:20). Paul was designated as a governmental leader of the Body of Christ, and as such was assigned to a much larger sphere of spiritual influence than most of us are. Because of how authority works, when we come into submission to an apostolic leader and are commissioned to serve their mission, we can operate with their authority. That is probably the broadest and most fundamental level of our spiritual covering.

How does spiritual authority work? When we pray, prophesy, and minister in the name of the Lord, we know that the Holy Spirit is the ultimate source of power and authority. In the same way that we are invited to co-labor with Him, God commissions angels to carry out His will. In Hebrews 1:14 it says of the angels, "Are they not ministering spirits sent out to render service for the sake of those who will receive salvation?" The angels are there to make sure that the sons and daughters of the King come into their destiny and that the mission of the Kingdom actually happens. What many of us don't realize is that we have a role in commissioning the angels. Psalm 103:19-22 says:

> *The Lord has established His throne in the heavens, and His sovereignty rules over all. Bless the Lord, you His angels, mighty in strength who perform His word, obeying the voice of His word. Bless, the Lord,*

all you His hosts, you who serve Him, doing His will. Bless the Lord all you works of His in all places of His dominion. Bless the Lord, oh my soul.

The angels heed the voice of His word, but the Church is His voice to declare that word on earth. I am proposing to you that the angels actually receive their commissioning from the prayers and prophecies of the saints. I don't think we have to tell the angels what to do; I think we just need to pray and prophesy in the Name of the Lord, and when they hear the word of the Lord they go out and perform it. But we can only declare a word of the Lord that commissions the angels if we are under authority and therefore have authority to send them. First Corinthians 11:1-10 mentions this in a discussion on spiritual covering:

Be imitators of me just as I also am of Christ. Now I praise you because you remember me in everything and hold firmly to the traditions just as I delivered them to you. But I want you to understand that Christ is the head of every man and the man is the head of a woman, and God is the head of Christ. Every man who has something on his head while praying or prophesying disgraces his head. But every woman who has her head uncovered while praying or prophesying disgraces her head, for she is one and the same as the woman who has her head shaved.... If a woman does not cover her head, let her also have her hair cut off, but if it is disgraceful for a woman to have her hair cut and her head shaved, let her cover her head. For a man ought not to have his head covered for he is the image and glory of God. But the woman is the glory of a man.... Therefore the woman ought to have a symbol of authority on her head because of the angels.

I'm aware that some teachers have come to extreme conclusions and used these verses to oppress women. That is not my goal at all. I just want to highlight that Paul says when a woman is praying or prophesying, she needs to have her head covered for the sake of the angels. Head coverings were a cultural sign of honor in the historic Corinthian church, and without one, a woman prophesying would be more or less saying she was standing on her own authority. Her prayers and prophecies wouldn't be recognized as coming from the Lord, because the angels are commissioned by those under the authority God has ordained.

It's a picture for us that we need to make sure we're submitted to those the Lord has placed in authority over us, because when the Bride of Christ is under authority, the angels recognize our authority and accomplish the words of our prayers and prophecies (see Ps. 103:20). When we submit to the mission of Heaven, we commission the angels to carry out the word of the Lord.

Do the angels always go out and answer everyone's prayers and prophecies? I don't believe they do, because I believe they recognize people who are under submission to an apostolic mission. This is just a theory, but I think sometimes people pray the right prayers when they're in trouble, but their life isn't in submission and so the situation doesn't change. They want to have the benefits of the Kingdom, but they don't want to serve the King. I don't mean they're going to hell, but they haven't recognized and submitted to the people that the Lord has delegated to have spiritual authority in their lives. So, according to First Corinthians 11, they don't have a symbol of authority on their head and the angels hear their prayers and say, "Still not commissioned."

The Lord recognizes His own authority. You can say "in Jesus' name" until you're purple, but the angels aren't going to recognize you unless you have a symbol of authority on your head. Whenever there's incongruity between the authority we're trying to take in a situation, and the authority we actually live under, the problem is going to go unsolved. Obviously that's a general statement and God can do whatever He wants to do. We've all seen God break whatever rule we preach. But there is a pattern that is clear in the Bible.

God has designed and commissioned a government for His Royal Priesthood. Its purpose is to equip the saints for the work of the ministry so we grow into the "measure of the stature of the fullness of Christ" (Eph. 4:13). It is amazing to me that when we begin to come under the vision of the leaders that God has put over us, that we start to experience blessings that we would never have experienced otherwise.

God is careful about whom He trusts with authority. He doesn't give authority to the most gifted people, but to those who have passed the tests, which give them the character to walk in spiritual authority. Let's look at a few biblical leaders whose personal breakthroughs brought corporate blessings.

— JOSEPH —

In Acts 7, before Stephen is stoned, he recounts a *"Reader's Digest"* version of the Old Testament to his accusers. He gives us a key insight into Israel's history.

> *There arose a king over Egypt who knew nothing about Joseph. It was he who took shrewd advantage of our race and mistreated our fathers so that they would expose their infants and they would not survive* (Act 7:18-19).

Notice that Stephen did not say there arose a king who knew not God and destroyed their race. Rather he said, "There arose a king who knew not Joseph." The implication is that Joseph's life somehow saved the Israelites from a life of death and despair. When Joseph died, Israel's covering was lost and the people of God were enslaved.

Joseph's personal victories became a corporate covering, but there is no victory without a battle. Battles are designed to free us from the prisons of life and take us to the palace of our destiny. Between the prison and the palace there is always a process that this warfare facilitates. The process is often better described as a trial. The trials of our life are designed to develop our character so that we can stay in the palace.

Let's take a closer look at the process toward prominence in Joseph's life: the first trial Joseph faces is the rejection of his brothers. At about seventeen, he has a couple of prophetic dreams. The dreams speak of him coming into a place of greatness where he sees his brothers and his parents serving him. He makes the mistake of announcing his destiny to his brothers, and they resent the idea of their shrimpy, arrogant brother ruling them. Already annoyed that their father favored Joseph like he was the firstborn, they decide one day that they can't handle him anymore and devise a plan to kill him. The oldest, Reuben, feeling this may be a little too extreme, talks them into throwing him into a pit instead. Just then, a train of slave-traders passes by, and the boys change their minds and sell Joseph for a profit instead.

Now, after that kind of rejection, many of us would face years of counseling. But Joseph has more trouble ahead of him. His sexual purity and integrity are going to be challenged. Joseph finds himself in Egypt, where Potiphar, an Egyptian officer of Pharaoh, buys him from the slave-traders. God is with Joseph and he rises to a place of prominence in Potiphar's house, eventually being put in charge of everything his boss owns. But Potiphar's wife tries to get Joseph to sleep with her. Day after day he refuses. She finally tries to rape him, but he escapes. Then she lies to her guards and accuses Joseph of sexually assaulting her. Potiphar believes her and sends Joe to prison.

Being wrongly accused is never fun, especially when we get put into prison for it. Most of us could get pretty bitter. Nevertheless, Joseph is faithful even in prison, God blesses him, and the chief jailer puts him in charge of the entire prison. As time in prison drags on, he gets the opportunity to interpret a couple of dreams for two of Pharaoh's servants who are also doing time. His gift of dream interpretation ultimately leads to his release from prison and his rise to rulership alongside Pharaoh himself. As Joseph begins his task as second in command, a seven-year famine plagues the known world. Through powerful prophetic foresight and godly insight, Joseph stores food for his nation with enough left over to sell to the surrounding nations that were also in crisis.

Notice that Joseph submitted to Pharaoh's authority, even though Pharaoh was a pagan leader. God could trust him with the position he had dreamt of years earlier because he had learned submission through his trials. He maintained that attitude in his position of authority. Submission to Pharaoh didn't mean he abandoned his identity and belief in God. It was precisely God's plans and ways that gave him the wisdom Pharaoh deferred to. Romans 13:1 states, "Let every soul be subject to the governing authorities. For there is no authority except from God, and the authorities that exist are appointed by God." Because Joseph recognized God's delegated authority and His way of testing, he proved himself worthy to walk in authority.

Joseph's extended family, who believe he is dead, come to Egypt for food. When his brothers find out he is alive, they beg for their own lives. He tells them that what they meant for evil, God used for good. He forgives them and invites them to move to Egypt so they will be safe from the famine. Seventy members of his family relocate to Egypt, where Pharaoh gives them the best land. They multiply and spread all over the nation, growing prosperous and remaining free until Joseph dies.

After Joseph dies, a new king comes into power. He becomes very jealous and afraid of the Israelites. He enslaves and kills thousands of them. Now, without Joseph, that's probably the treatment they would have gotten in the first place. They were shepherds, and Egyptians hated shepherds, but because of Joseph's covering, they were treated like he deserved to be treated. The Israelites lived a life of incredible blessing during the years of Joseph's rulership, not because they deserved it, but because Joseph did!

Joseph was in a powerful position when he decided the fate of his family in Egypt. Joseph had gone through the tests of character and his personal victories were many: he believed God would fulfill the dreams of his life, even though circumstances were against him; he submitted to authority, was faithful and trusted God through everything; he stayed clear from sexual sin, and he was willing to forgive his brothers. His successes allowed him to become a corporate covering and a trusted general in the kingdom to protect all those who came under him (see Gen. 37–48).

— DAVID —

This same process can be seen in the life of David in First Samuel, chapter 17. David is sent by his father to bring lunch to his brothers, who are fighting against the Philistines. A giant Philistine soldier named Goliath stands in the battlefield and starts cursing, taunting and mocking the Israelite armies. Goliath finally comes to the point when he says,

> *Choose a man for yourselves and let him come down to me. If he is able to fight with me and kill me, then we will become your servants; but if I prevail against him and kill him, then you shall become our servants and serve us* (1 Samuel 17:8b,9).

(On a side note, giants in Scripture are often a symbol of spiritual principalities. Goliath's challenge is a good example of how spiritual authority works. If the principality is unseated, then everyone that was under its influence will come under the influence of whatever replaces it. Here, if someone kills the giant, all the Philistines will serve Israel, but if that person loses the battle, all of Israel will be enslaved to the Philistines.)

David is up for the task because, like Joseph, he has been faithful in a place of obscurity. He has been doing a remarkable job taking care of a herd of sheep on the edge of the wilderness. Once again, this is the key to obtaining spiritual authority: submission until promotion. Little did he know that the challenges he faced while protecting his flock would prepare him for his day of destiny.

Before he can fight Goliath, again like Joseph, he must first endure his brothers' ridicule. Those of us who aspire to leadership must realize that we will face what Joseph and David did from their brothers. Like David and Joseph's brothers, people who have no vision live their lives in the bondage of their own frailties and sins. They persecute anyone who has a vision, has conquered fear, or lives their life above sin rather than under it. This persecution takes place because it is easy to feel all right about their bondage as long as everybody they know is in bondage too—misery loves company. If someone starts to get victory in the same circumstances that others are failing in, it takes away their excuses and calls them to give an account for the inconsistencies in their character.

Scripture says that David, before he fought the giant, left "his baggage with the baggage keeper" (1 Sam. 17:22). While that wasn't necessarily a character test for him, I believe it's mentioned as a significant detail because he is modeling how we should face our challenges. David didn't go into battle without first unloading anything that could hinder him. Similarly, we shouldn't plunge into confrontation with the enemy without first letting God confront any unresolved sin or issues in our heart. I find the most important things we do in our lives are often done in private. Watch out for people who have a public victory without a private one.

David finally knocks Goliath down with a stone and kills him with Goliath's own sword. The very weapon that was meant to destroy David became the weapon of choice in the hand of this great warrior.

Because David took down the champion of the Philistines, the battle ended. David's personal victory became a corporate blessing, bringing all of Israel peace.

— FAVOR WITH THE INVISIBLE —

One of the principles that is important for us to understand here is that physical obedience brings spiritual release. Paul said that the natural is first, then the spiritual (see 1 Cor. 15:46). We have been investigating the lives of people who passed their character tests, completing the process of promotion in the natural (visible) realm of life, which then resulted in gaining authority in the spirit (invisible) realm. Much of the church hardly acknowledges the invisible realm at all, much less realizes the implications that it has on our daily lives. The invisible kingdom that lies within us and around us is more powerful than the visible world that is perceived with our natural eyes. We are either benefited or befuddled by the invisible world, depending on how we relate to it.

A great example of how the invisible realm powerfully affects the visible realm is in the lives of Moses and Joshua when Joshua was commissioned by Moses to take his soldiers and go down in the valley to fight Amalek. Moses went up on the mountain and held up his hands.

Whenever Moses would get tired and drop his arms, Joshua would begin to lose. When Moses lifted his hands up, Joshua would win. It became clear to them that Joshua's victory was directly tied to Moses raising his hands, so they put a leader on each side of Moses to help support his arms. Joshua won the battle and all was well in Israel that day (see Exod. 17:8-13).

If we don't understand how to gain favor with the invisible world, we build bigger armies, develop better strategies, and buy more powerful weapons, yet we still lose! It just never occurs to us that if we support (honor) our leaders, we inherit their victories.

God raises up men and women like Moses, David, and Joseph, not for their own glory, but for the good of His people. Those who have proven faithful He entrusts with authority to govern His people. As the people of God come into a place of submission to their leaders who have won their personal victories, they become heirs of their leader's spoil. Through inheritance, they receive blessing that they have not earned. Because many in the Body of Christ today don't realize this, a couple of things have happened.

The first is there are so many people in the Body of Christ who have chosen to fight battles that have already been won by someone else. Many of these battles have resulted in unnecessary wounds and, in extreme cases, even death. These are needless casualties of war. There is no glory in scars that occur in a battle to take ground that God already occupies.

The second problem is that many people call themselves leaders who still have not won their personal victories. They have deceived themselves into thinking they are a covering for the saints. The truth of the matter is that these battles that have been lost in the personal lives of so-called "shepherds" have resulted in slavery in the people who are gathered to them. When areas of their lives are not in submission to God, they are in submission to something else, whether it is themselves or some other idol. If people follow them, they end up submitting to the same idol. This is how spiritual authority works. So many believers are blind to this principle, which as we saw in David's story, Goliath understood perfectly.

Paul speaks into this issue when he said to Timothy:

> *An overseer, then, must be above reproach, the husband of one wife, temperate, prudent, respectable, hospitable, able to teach, not addicted to wine or pugnacious, but gentle, peaceable, free from the love of money. He must be one who manages his own household well, keeping his children under control with all dignity (but if a man does not know how to manage his own household, how will he take care of the church of God?), and not a new convert, so that he will not become conceited and fall into the condemnation incurred by the devil* (1 Timothy 3:2-6).

Of course, this does not mean that a leader cannot have a bad day. It does mean, however, that they have no business leading if they are having a bad life. Lifestyle sins do disqualify people from leading until there's repentance that is tested in the furnace of perseverance. Perseverance is the ability to hold our course over time in the face of opposition. The element of time cannot be ignored in a leader's test of repentance. Nothing supersedes bad character, not even educational degrees, spiritual gifts, experiences, or the people we know. Nothing will make up for the bondage of sin. Victories of the past cannot override the sins of the present. Fallen leaders who have a lifestyle of sin must come under a true covering while they rebuild their own lives. This covering provides a greenhouse effect that gives people an opportunity to recover in a safe environment.

— COVERING ONE ANOTHER —

The final thing I want to mention on the subject of spiritual covering is that Paul instructs us many times in his letters to submit to one another as to Christ. There is an element of spiritual covering that is preserved as we honor our covenant with the Body of Christ and with one another as brothers and sisters in the Lord. The Lord calls us His Body because every member is dependent on the other and every choice we

214 THE SUPERNATURAL WAYS OF ROYALTY

make affects the whole. If we choose to honor and serve the Body of Christ, we preserve the connection that brings life, blessing, and protection to us.

In the Book of Acts, chapter 27, Paul is in a ship about to wreck. Even though Paul has already prophesied that there shall be no loss of life and only the ship will be lost, some of the sailors decide that they are going to escape in lifeboats. When Paul discovers that some men are planning to escape, he says, "If they leave the ship we will ALL die" (Acts 27:31). We need to realize that as believers we are partners in destiny. Individually, we are members of one another. Leaders especially need to understand that their actions and attitudes have ramifications that are magnified many times over. The good news is that the more we line up with God's plan, the more authority and power are released through us to establish the Kingdom of God. Like David and Joseph, if we pursue godly character and submit to the authority God has set up, we can be trusted with the royal authority that will commission the angels to push back hell and pull Heaven down!

Chapter 17

PRESERVING THE PLANET

*It's hard to give people "Heaven by the half acre" while believing that
"things are going to hell in a hand basket."*
– Jack Taylor

— THE DOOMSDAY PROPHETS —

As a royal priesthood and a holy nation, it is our privilege and responsibility to intercede on behalf of the world before our King. It has been said that God does nothing in the affairs of men except they pray. Prayer is the catalyst for worldwide transformation. It incites the angels, restrains the darkness, and releases nations into their destiny. It is this key to revival which builds the bridge between what should be and what will be. This book is dedicated to the purpose of revival.

The devil knows the power of prayer and cannot stop us from praying. But he is the master of deception. He tries to convince us that his destructive schemes are "Acts of God" so that the people of God will not release the arsenal of Heaven against him! Unfortunately, satan has been more successful at deceiving the saints recently than he has for decades. One of the ways he has subtly crept into our society and even the Church has been through misdirected leaders preaching the "wrath of God."

In the last decade the "Doomsday" prophets seemed to have come out of hibernation. In 1997, my own parents moved out of the San Francisco Bay area to avoid the wrath of a great earthquake prophesied to strike southern California. The earthquake was going to destroy

Hollywood for its immoral pollution of the media and San Francisco for its homosexual perversion. The word also predicted that Northern California would become "ocean front property."

My Mom and Dad relocated to Lake Tahoe near Nevada, hoping to find a prophetic "no-fly" zone. Just about the time my folks got settled, several prophets began to prophesy about an upcoming international famine. This became known around the world as the "Y2K bug." This bug was going to judge us for making our intellect a god. It was the perfect "God Scheme." The whole plan was hidden by our foolish confidence in man's brilliance. It seemed that the Lord had blinded every computer nerd in the world, keeping them from discovering in time that we would all be starving over the lack of a digit. What a way to go! There would be rioting in the streets; people would be fighting off the temptation to cannibalize their neighbors and children! Businesses and governments would crumble next. Some even predicted this would start the "Mother of all Wars." People streamed en masse to buy generators and guns to protect their food in the "name of the Lord." Needless to say, these preparations proved to be pointless, and my parents are still driving for hours to reach the ocean.

September 11, 2001, will forever be branded in the minds of Americans as a monument to murder. America woke up to the sounds of people screaming, many of them on fire as they exited the black smoke of a man-made hell. Explosions could be heard in the background as buildings crumbled and thousands were trapped in would-be tombs. Weeping and wailing were heard for miles as people wandered aimlessly through the streets looking for their loved ones. Many jumped to their deaths from these flaming infernos. Deep sadness and fear blanketed the whole earth as the news spread. Everywhere, people were crying out for mercy for those who were counted among the missing. People were glued to their TV sets, praying, hoping, and believing that life would emerge from the rubble.

Although the "prophets of doom" had not prophesied this disaster, declarations of darkness began to emerge from what was supposed to be the "house of hope." They came even before we could ask ourselves why such a mindless act of horror would be perpetrated on the lives of the many innocent who died that day. Many of the prophets of God began to proclaim words of judgment for the sins of the nation. Their thesis was that God had caused this tragedy due to His hatred of sin. Can you imagine the grief that beset those who had lost loved ones? They were confronted by an angry God who wanted to kill more people. Just as Jesus said, "In the last days the love of many will grow cold" (Matt. 24:12).

— TRUE RIGHTEOUSNESS IS SALT —

It is true that immorality, idolatry, abortion, and murder are just a few of the cancers that revival must address. But I believe the gravest sin in our nation today is the chill of frozen hearts that are resident in spiritual fathers who no longer love. These misled believers spread fear, destroy hope, and castrate people's faith. They have somehow lost fellowship with the Comforter, choosing rather to embrace the contradictory and confusing "gospel of bad news."

Jesus told us, "You are the salt of the earth; but if the salt has become tasteless, how can it be made salty again? It is no longer good for anything, except to be thrown out and trampled under foot by men" (Matt. 5:13). In Jesus' day, they didn't have refrigerators to store their food. Salt was the primary means by which they preserved their meat and poultry. Through this analogy, the Lord is teaching us that the Church is the element in society that preserves the culture from the wrath of God and the destruction of evil forces. A great example of this is Joseph, who as we saw in the last chapter, released a corporate blessing through his righteous life. His presence in Egypt caused the Israelites and the Egyptians to be spared from a worldwide famine.

Jesus also said that when salt becomes tasteless, it is not good for anything except to be walked on by men. In other words, the people of the day would taste the salt and if it was no longer salty, they knew that it would not keep their food from spoiling. It's important to remember that Jesus is not really talking about preserving meat, but describing the

Body of Christ. What does it mean to become tasteless? It implies that we have stopped preserving the world. We have become tasteless when we prophesy against the people we are supposed to be preserving. This became very clear to me in the midst of the storm of prophecies predicting disastrous events in North America.

I began to seek the Lord with a new zeal for the truth. As I lay on the floor praying, the Holy Spirit started talking to me.

He said, "I don't destroy cities because of the abundance of the wicked. I only destroy them if there is a lack of righteous people."

Then He took me to Genesis 18 and 19. Here Abraham negotiates with God to save Sodom if there were only ten righteous people.

The Lord said to me, "Ask Me how I can tell if there are enough righteous souls in a city to save it."

So I did.

He answered, "I prophesy a word of judgment. Then I wait to see how many of My people will rise up and cry out for mercy. In this way, mercy triumphs over judgment" (James 2:13).

Then God asked me another question, "Was Lot's wife righteous or wicked?"

Although I had preached for years that Lot's wife was wicked for looking back to Sin-City, somehow that just did not seem like the correct answer at that moment.

I found myself saying, "I don't know."

God continued, "What was her name?"

I responded, "I don't know."

"What was Abraham's wife's name?" He asked.

"Sarah," I answered. (I was sure of that one.)

"That's right," God said, "So she had an identity apart from Abraham." Now I was getting it! Lot's wife was not named because her identity was attached to Lot's righteousness!

"That's right," the Lord said, and continued, "Was Lot righteous or wicked?"

"Righteous," I replied.

"What did she turn into when she looked back?" Jesus asked.

"Salt," I said.

"What is salt?" God asked.

"A preservative," I said.

"Yes! She lived with a mantle of intercession. She knew they were preserving that city."

Finally, I understood that her body turning into a pillar of salt was a prophetic metaphor for the role that she had played in the city. Because Lot and his wife were the "salt" or "preservative" of Sodom, they were preservation for the city. Then they had a chance to escape judgment when the Lord finally decided to release fire and brimstone. Lot's wife simply made a bad choice in a time of deliverance.

"She could not let go when I did. Her own ministry killed her." God explained.

This point is clarified in Luke 17:"On that day, the one who is on the housetop and whose goods are in the house must not go down to take them out; and likewise the one who is in the field must not turn back. Remember Lot's wife. Whoever seeks to keep his life will lose it, and whoever loses his life will preserve it" (31-33).

Then God reminded me of the words of Jeremiah,

> *Roam to and fro through the streets of Jerusalem, and look now and take note, and seek in her open squares; if you can find a man, if there is one who does justice, who seeks truth, then I will pardon her* (Jeremiah 5:1).

He also brought the words of Ezekiel to mind:"I searched for a man among them who would build up the wall and stand in the gap before Me for the land, so that I would not destroy it; but I found no one" (Ezek. 22:30).

It is no coincidence that at the same time many of God's prophets are speaking words of destruction, the largest move of intercession in the history of the world is rising up calling for mercy. We must remember that although God does use words of judgment at times to rally His intercessors, His heart is to extend mercy. God takes no pleasure in the death of the wicked (see Ezek. 18:23). We should cry out for God to heal our cities until the angels carry us out of them as they did in the days of Lot.

— A Lack of Faith and Distorted Core Values —

Despite the fact that God uses judgment words at times, I don't believe that most of the recent words of judgment are a warning from our Father at all but instead are the fruit of two major problems in the church. First, there is an underlying lack of faith in many Christians that keeps them from believing that God will actually have a "spotless bride"; second, many saints have wrong core values, which distort their world view and infect their ministry.

Core values are the lenses that determine the way we see life. They are interpreters of the events of our world. When something happens to us or around us, our core values dictate what we think about it. Our core values determine which events in life we attribute to God, to the devil, or to nature itself.

A great example of how wrong core values can affect our lives and ministries is seen in the area of intercession. Many intercessors have been neutralized because they have believed a lie and therefore develop a wrong core value that says, "Disaster breeds humility, and humility gives birth to repentance, which in turn fuels revival." When we see the world through this lens, we stop praying for deliverance and pray for endurance instead. I wonder how many times we have let the devil wreak havoc in our lives or the lives of those around us because we thought God was testing us.

It is important to understand that most revivals didn't begin with a catastrophe. For example, the Azusa Street revival began with prayer.

The Jesus movement didn't begin with disaster nor did the Charismatic renewal. The Welsh revival had nothing to do with tragedy. The Toronto and Brownsville revivals didn't begin because of calamity.

In fact, throughout most of the Bible, disaster created quite the opposite response. In the Book of Numbers, God caused some of the leaders of Israel to be swallowed up by an earthquake. In keeping with His nature, Moses begged for mercy twice in this chapter on behalf of his people. The bitterness of the Israelites who survived, grew worse with each disaster. They blamed Moses for the loss of their family members and did everything but repent (16:23-41). In the Book of Revelation, we have the same principle. Plagues are poured out on the people, but they do not repent and instead, "blaspheme the God of heaven" (16:10-11).

We have all met people who have lost a child or a loved one in an untimely manner. Many of them go through life bitter with God over their loss. Others question the reality of a loving God when they look around and see people starving. Although God can and often does turn around a bad situation and use it for good, it is still, "the kindness of God that leads to repentance." (Rom. 2:4). It's the devil that wants to kill, steal and destroy. He is the master of twisting the Scriptures so that we allow Him a place to come in and carry out his devious plan. Remember that this is the same guy who used the Bible to try to convince Jesus to commit suicide:

> *Then the devil took Him into the holy city and had Him stand on the pinnacle of the temple, and said to Him, "If You are the Son of God, throw Yourself down; for it is written,*
>
> *'He will command His angels concerning You; and*
> *on their hands they will bear You up,*
> *so that You will not strike Your foot against a stone'"* (Matthew 4:5,6).

— RE-PRESENTING CHRIST —

Not only is the Church preservation (salt), but also we are light. In the Book of Matthew Jesus said, "You are the light of the world. A city set on a hill cannot be hidden" (Matt. 5:14). What does it mean to be light, and what is it that we are illuminating? We are shedding light on the nature of God, which is how He thinks and acts in the affairs of men. We are the revelation (light) of the Father and His love letter to the world. We re-present Christ to the lost. The world looks to us to understand world events through the eyes of God. When we misrepresent our Heavenly Father, the world gets a warped perspective of God.

James and John are a good example of how many misrepresent God. They wanted to call fire down to consume a city, but Jesus said to them, "You don't know what spirit you are of" (Luke 9:54-55). It is interesting to me that this was the same John who wrote to the Beloved and exhorted us, "Not to believe every spirit, but to test the spirits to see whether they are from God, because many false prophets have gone out into the world" (1 John 4:1). I imagine that he received the revelation that even Jesus' own apostles could be influenced by hell through his own experience of listening to the wrong spirit.

Notice how his exhortation continues in the same chapter: "Beloved, let us love one another…There is no fear in love; but perfect love casts out fear, because fear involves punishment, and the one who fears is not perfected in love" (1 John 4:18). These verses were written in the context of testing the spirits. In other words, we test the spirits by examining them in light of the virtues of love. When we read these virtues that are spelled out in the letter to the Corinthians (1 Cor. 13) and understand that fear has no place in love, we find ourselves wondering what spirit is encouraging these judgment prophecies. The greatest tragedy is that the revelation the world receives from these voices causes them to believe that our Father is an angry God who is looking for an opportunity to punish people.

Jesus said, "…If then the light that is in you is darkness, how great is the darkness!" (Matt. 6:23). If we are the light of the world and we are speaking and prophesying against the people who are already lost in darkness, how great is the darkness! In the same way, when we represent God as someone who wants to destroy America because 40 million babies have been aborted in our country, we perpetuate the very problem that we are trying to cure. People are killing their babies because they don't know or understand the love of the Father. Does it make sense to tell people that God is so angry that we are killing our young that He is going to kill all of us? Is our Father so single-dimensional in His being that He only has one response to anything man does wrong?

The way in which many believers reflect God to the world reminds me more of my stepfather than my Heavenly Father. Can you imagine the negative impact it would have on your daughter if she came to you to tell you that she had an abortion, and in response, you flipped out and tried to kill her? If you react out of rage, I would suggest that your lack of love is a large part of her decision to have the abortion in the first place.

When we communicate to the world about the God they have yet to meet, it is essential that we communicate light, life, and love. Love doesn't punish or spread fear. Our Abba Father does grieve over the sins of the world, but every time we see the heartless acts of destruction that deeply wound the heart of God, we must remember the depths of God's desire to share love. The nature of love is that it requires us to be able to choose. If God took away our choice, people could only behave the way God programmed them to. Wars would cease, hunger would end, and poverty would only be an ancient memory of years gone by. But along with their disappearance, the desperate cry of the human heart that beats with passion for a loving relationship with the most beautiful Being in the entire universe would be gone, too.

Day after day, a loving Creator looks down on a broken planet longing for the day when the object of His affection will walk hand in hand with Him into indescribable beauty in the halls of eternity. In the meantime destruction continues, not because God is angry with man, but rather because men choose to kill, steal, and destroy. This is the fruit of those who have chosen the wrong lover (satan).

In the midst of all this darkness there is an incredible hope growing. The day after the Twin Towers were destroyed I had a vision. In the vision I saw what all of us saw hundreds of times—the towers of fire falling like sand castles to the ground. But this time, in the vision, something was different. There was a loud voice yelling behind the towers, *"The blood of the martyrs; the blood of the martyrs!"* What happened next in the vision was amazing. Cracks began to form over the entire earth almost as if they were repercussions of the explosions. Water began to flow all over the world. Then another voice began to shout, *"The fountains of the deep are open; the fountains of the deep are open!"*

I asked God, "What does this mean?"

He said, "The knowledge of the glory of the Lord shall cover the earth as the waters cover the sea!"

Jesus said, "Truly, truly, I say to you, unless a grain of wheat falls into the earth and dies, it remains alone; but if it dies, it bears much fruit" (John 12:24). I believe that because God is a God of redemption, He makes sure that the ramification of Christians being killed for their faith is mass spiritual conversions. Although God did not cause 9-11 in judgment of the world, He is able to use this horrific circumstance to bring about His purposes.

Paul said, *"Where sin abounds, grace did much more abound"* (Rom. 5:20 KJV). If the level of sin determines the depths of grace, then our country must be poised for an incredible move of God.

Meanwhile, a hateful enemy is stalking a wounded and desperate people. He is seeking to paralyze us with fear and demoralize us with his arrogant boasts of destructive predications. Yet still, the future belongs to those who pray. Prayer is the bridge between what should be and what will be. The diligent prayer of a righteous people will ultimately determine the destiny of our children. Therefore it is our responsibility to leave to those yet to be born a world in revival as their inheritance. Hanging in the balance of eternity is the ultimate climax of creation—the kingdoms of this world becoming the Kingdom of our God.

Name: _____

Date: _____

— PRINCE AND PAUPER TEST —

We are sons and daughters of God Himself; therefore we are not "paupers" in the kingdom, but "princes" and "princesses." This test is designed to help you grow in the attributes of royalty, which have been defined and discussed throughout this book.

As you read the questions, the reality of your true identity will be revealed and you will begin to question how you act, and why you might believe certain lies about yourself. The test is designed to make you aware of the areas in your life in which you need assistance. The point is not to reflect what you do, but how you perceive yourself. Through this revelatory knowledge, you will be able to commence on a journey to renew your mind and break your "pauper" mentality.

In order for this test to be helpful, it is necessary to be as honest with yourself as possible. Answer the questions in such a way that reflects who and how you are most often—not how you feel or react on the worst or best day of your life.

PART 1

— SCORING KEY —
0=Never 1=Seldom 2=Sometimes 3=Often 4=Very Often 5=Always

_____ 1. I tend to have a sarcastic sense of humor that cuts people down.

_____ 2. I like to buy things on sale or at discount department stores.

_____ 3. I struggle with feelings of inadequacy.

_____ Subtotal

0=Never   1=Seldom   2=Sometimes   3=Often   4=Very Often   5=Always

____ 4. I find myself secretly competing with the people around me.

____ 5. I often look in the mirror.

____ 6. I compare myself to others.

____ 7. I want the "underdog" to win.

____ 8. I believe God favors the underdog.

____ 9. I am uncomfortable around rich and/ or successful people.

____ 10. I tend to build cases against people who seem successful or have power over me.

____ 11. I tell others of significant people I am friends with or important projects that I have worked on or am involved with.

____ 12. I overwork and feel really low when I am not accomplishing something.

____ 13. I am on several committees and volunteer for anything that has a sense of validation, without respect to my own gifts.

____ 14. I am compelled to be friends with the most important person in any organization that I am involved in.

____ 15. I don't like to set goals because when I don't reach them, it makes me feel like I have failed.

____ 16. I repeat myself, dramatize, over emphasize, exaggerate and/or lie during conversations to make my point.

____ Subtotal

— SCORING KEY —

0=Never 1=Seldom 2=Sometimes 3=Often 4=Very Often 5=Always

_____ 17. I become overly attached in an unhealthy way to anyone who gives me attention or takes an interest in me.

_____ 18. I like to give things away, but I am almost embarrassed to receive gifts from people.

_____ 19. I spend a lot of time wondering what people think about me.

_____ 20. My opinion is easily changed to please others.

_____ 21. I tend to have the opposite opinion of the leader in most environments. If they say "black," I almost feel obligated to argue "white."

_____ 22. The friends I feel the most comfortable with are usually broken people.

_____ 23. When I chose a team to work with me, I chose people who I deem as weaker than myself.

_____ 24. I don't like to be around, and tend to reject, people who have a different opinion from mine.

_____ 25. I don't just share my opinion, I feel driven to argue with or manipulate people into agreeing with me.

_____ 26. When people don't agree with me, I take it personally and tend to think that they have rejected me.

_____ 27. I need to be the most important person in the room and/or be in control to be happy.

_____ 28. People say I am obsessed with being right.

_____ Subtotal

— SCORING KEY: —

0=Never   1=Seldom   2=Sometimes   3=Often   4=Very Often   5=Always

_____ 29. I struggle with fears, especially the fear of rejection
and failure.

_____ 30. I worry a lot, especially about the future.

_____ 31. I feel like something is about to go wrong.

_____ 32. I struggle with forgiving people.

_____ 33. I am easily offended.

_____ 34. I feel that the failures and bad experiences in my life
were not my fault.

_____ 35. I feel anger and/or rage right below the surface of
my being.

_____ 36. I feel like people are rushing me when I am talking
and/or explaining myself to them.

_____ 37. I have felt misunderstood most of my life.

_____ 38. Disgruntled and dissatisfied people tend to tell me
their problems.

_____ 39. My sex drive and/or eating habits seem to be out
of control.

_____ 40. I sleep more than normal and still find myself tired
a lot.

_____ Subtotal

Grading Instructions:

Please add the points from each subtotals. Record your score on the
line below. Continue answering the following questions.

_____ Total points for Part 1

PART 2

— SCORING KEY —

0=Never   1=Seldom   2=Sometimes   3=Often   4=Very Often   5=Always

_____ 1. I enjoy investing in people and seeing them outgrow me.

_____ 2. I allow people to have the glory in conversations. Example: A person says, "I have been so busy." I respond, "What have you been doing?" instead of saying, "I have been busy too."

_____ 3. I like being around free thinkers and creative people.

_____ 4. I like to solve problems with people but not for them.

_____ 5. I like to create an environment where people learn to think for themselves.

_____ 6. I love myself and sense God's pleasure in me.

_____ 7. I feel comfortable around almost everyone.

_____ 8. I tend to attract important and successful people.

_____ 9. I can eat at nice restaurants, stay in nice places, and have nice things without feeling guilty.

_____ 10. I don't do things for the sake of image but only because I personally value them.

_____ 11. I enjoy empowering people more than I like having power over people.

_____ 12. I love diversity in the people I have relationships with.

_____ Subtotal

— SCORING KEY —

0=Never 1=Seldom 2=Sometimes 3=Often 4=Very Often 5=Always

_____ 13. I tend to choose people to be on my team who have other perspectives and different points of view from my own.

_____ 14. I easily rejoice in other people's victories.

_____ 15. I give things to people not just because they need them but rather to honor people who deserve it.

_____ 16. I am motivated by the vision I have for my life.

_____ 17. I am hard to offend.

_____ 18. I dream about making a dramatic impact on the world.

_____ 19. I expect people to like me.

_____ 20. I initiate making contact with people first instead of waiting for them to come to me

_____ 21. One of my main purposes in life is to help other people discover and obtain their dreams.

_____ 22. I am a self-starter.

_____ 23. I bring out the best in people.

_____ 24. I think of better ways to do things.

_____ 25. I am a good listener. I look people in the eyes when they are talking to me.

_____ 26. Joy often overtakes me and I catch myself smiling for no obvious reason.

_____ 27. People tend to follow me no matter what I am doing.

_____ Subtotal

— SCORING KEY —

0=Never 1=Seldom 2=Sometimes 3=Often 4=Very Often 5=Always

_____ 28. I like to receive nice things from people.

_____ 29. People stop using bad language, stop complaining and/or clean up their act when I am around, even if I haven't required it of them.

_____ 30. I spend a lot of time thinking about and being thankful for the good things that have happened.

_____ 31. I love people easily and I am patient with them by nature.

_____ 32. I feel like I am in control of my natural passions including eating, sleeping, and sex.

_____ 33. I enjoy relaxing and find it easy to rest most of the time.

_____ 34. I am aware of the Holy Spirit and Jesus talking to me throughout the day.

_____ 35. I set goals for the areas of my life where I have responsibility.

_____ 36. I have a good idea what my strengths and/or gifts are as well as my weaknesses.

_____ 37. When I fail, I take the responsibility for it without blaming others.

_____ 38. I love being alive and look forward to the future.

_____ 39. I like to take risks and experience new things.

_____ 40. I go out of my way to expose myself to the needs of the poor and minister to those broken in heart and spirit. I have compassion for people less fortunate than myself.

_____ Subtotal

GRADING INSTRUCTIONS:

Please add the points from each subtotal in Part 2 only. Record your score on the line below.

_____ Total points for Part 2

Final Grading Instructions:

Complete the following:

Subtract Part 1 of your score from Part 2.
This becomes your final score.

Your score may be a negative number.

Score from Part 2:_____

Minus

Score from Part 1:_____

Final Score:_____

Look at the following chart and find the place on the graph that correctly corresponds to your final score and mark it with an X. This number is an indication of the attributes of royalty that you currently possess. Take this test again in a few months to check the progress you are making toward reaching your royal identity.

GRAPH

Pauper -200 -175 -150 -125 -100 -75 -50 -25 0 +25
+50 +75 +100 +125 +150 +175 +200 **Prince**

IN THE BEGINNING

Some new friends reading this book may have no idea how to get started in a life with Jesus. I would like to take a moment now and explain where to begin.

The Bible makes it clear that all of us are in need of a Savior—someone to pay for our sins so we don't have to live a life of bondage and torment. Jesus died on the Cross for us and He also died as us. He took on the penalty for all we have ever done wrong and ever will do wrong. Jesus wants to do more than forgive us; He wants to give us a brand-new life in the Kingdom of God—right now on this earth. He also desires to take us to Heaven when we pass from this life into the next.

As if that isn't enough, there is more! He promised that when we ask Him into our hearts we will be "born again" and become a new creation. He gives us a new life with a new heart and a new mind. You have read about these promises in this book.

What do you have to do to begin this amazing life with God? Good question. The answer: You need to be willing to give the leadership role of your life to Jesus and be serious about following Him. You need to acknowledge that you have sinned and that you need His help to change. You need to ask Him to forgive you, and you need to forgive everyone who has hurt you.

If you are willing to do these things to follow Jesus, please pray this prayer:

"Jesus, I have done a lot of things wrong in my life and need you to forgive me. I am sorry for the life that I have led without you in my heart. From now on I want to follow you and let you be in charge of my entire life. I am ready to forsake my old life and take on your life, your ways, and your desires. I will forgive everyone who has harmed or hurt me and allow them to live free from my revenge. I ask you to send your Holy Spirit into my life and baptize me with your love and power. Amen!

Now find a good church where you can grow, and go there as often as possible. Look for someone who is mature in God to mentor you—sometimes this happens naturally in home groups. Read your Bible daily (begin in the Book of John) and ask the Holy Spirit to teach you as you read. Take time to pray every day, listening for Jesus to speak to you as you seek Him. Last of all, share your life and faith with others.

May the King of Glory meet you in the palace of your dreams as you begin your new life in the Kingdom of God!

Love,

Kris Vallotton
Bethel Church
933 College View Drive
Redding, CA 96003
WWW.KVMINISTRIES.COM

A CALL TO WAR:
BASIC TRAINING FOR THE PROPHETIC MINISTRY

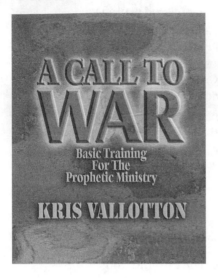

In a practical and easy-to-understand style, this manual presents the prophetic ministry in a way that "demystifies" the Gift of Prophecy and allows every believer to realize that God can and will speak through YOU!

"A Call to War" brings together the elements of teaching and practical application that will build a strong foundation for signs and wonders to follow.

Subjects include:

- Learning to Hear The Voice of God
- How the Gifts Grow in Our Lives
- The Purpose of Prophetic Ministry
- The Difference Between The Office of Prophet and The Gift of Prophecy
- Prophetic Etiquette
- False Prophets

Whether a Pastor or a leader wanting to develop prophetic ministry in your church, or an individual who simply wants to grow in this precious, life-changing gift of the Holy Spirit, "A Call to War" is a must-have tool that will bring life and wage war on the powers of darkness!

"A CALL TO WAR" is available at www.kvministries.com, or www.ibethel.org

or by calling Bethel Church, Media Department 530-246-6000

BETHEL SCHOOL OF
SUPERNATURAL MINISTRY

Bethel School of Supernatural Ministry is dedicated to worldwide transformation through spiritual revival. We are training and equipping the Body of Christ to bring the love of God and the power of the Holy Spirit into the darkest places of the planet and establish Holy Spirit fortifications, resulting in the kingdom of this world becoming the Kingdom of our God.

BSSM is more than a school, it's a Holy Spirit journey into the realm of the impossible, a heavenly adventure where no one dare travel without God. In this haven of love, you will learn how to minister with power, and walk in signs and wonders.

BSSM's mission is to equip and deploy revivalists who passionately pursue worldwide transformation within their God-given spheres of influence.

Pastor Kris Vallotton - Senior Overseer

Pastor Bill Johnson - President

For more information, visit our Website at: www.ibethel.org or call 530-246-6000.

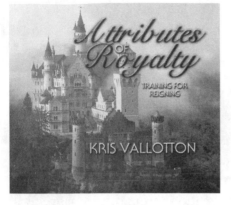

ATTRIBUTES OF ROYALTY

Kris unearths the mysteries of our noble lineage, reminding us that as the people of God, we are called to be a Royal Priesthood. He takes us on a journey through the King's palace for prince and princess training at its best. You will learn how Royalty thinks, how they behave and why they have authority. You'll also come to realize how the destructive nature of pauperhood has reduced the great commission down to something less powerful and more palatable. You'll receive insights from the life of David, Solomon, and Esther and be struck by the nations that were discipled in ancient enemy lands through the stately influence of Daniel and Joseph. But most of all, you will discover the yearning that you possess, deep within your soul, to become sons and daughters of the King.

DEVELOPING A LEGACY

If you're not building a legacy, you are developing a monument unto yourself. God wants to create a family, a legacy, a culture of true discipleship where people are loved and cared for, corrected and directed, nurtured and embraced—not a monument! You were created as a Christian to disciple and be discipled.

These and many other titles available at www.kvministries.com,
or www.ibethel.org,
or phone us at 530-246-6000.

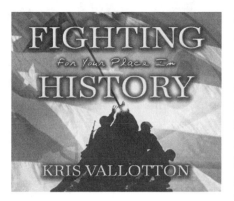

FIGHTING FOR YOUR PLACE IN HISTORY

This teaching will equip you to discover your divine call and propel you into your place in history. This message is a "must hear" for everyone lacking purpose in their life. Discover how "the dogs of doom stand at your doors of destiny." What are the factors that are keeping you from being all that you can be? How can you break free from these powerful forces and go where no one has ever gone before? The answers may surprise you!

FOR THE LOVE OF GOD

This is a journey into the heart of God viewed through the eyes of a boy and his grandfather. You'll laugh and cry yourself into a new place of love, and find a fresh place of passion as you discover the One who has been waiting for all eternity just to dance this last dance with you. This message will surprise you.

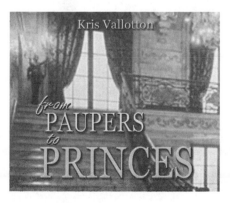

FROM PAUPERS TO PRINCES

This powerful message is taken from Kris' personal journey out of a life of insignificance, into a place of leadership. His words will confront the "pauper" and call out the "prince" in you. Kris explores the destructive nature of the "pauper" mentality and brings wisdom to escape its claws.

PURITY

In this message Pastor Kris Vallotton explores the battle over your virginity and equips you with some powerful weapons to win. This message also provides hope for those who have lost this battle and leads them back to victory.

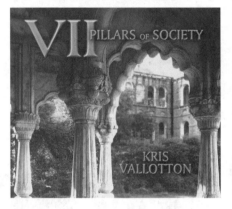

SEVEN PILLARS OF SOCIETY

Awakened in the middle of the night with instructions from the Lord to write down the "Seven Pillars of Society," Pastor Kris Vallotton struggled in the twilight to find pen and paper. He had no clue that what he was about to receive would forever revolutionize the role of the church on the earth and restore the desecrated fabric of our land. Like a spiritual archaeologist, Kris unearthed the ancient foundations of the God-given virtues that cement civilization into a cohesive, global community.

These and many other titles available at www.kvministries.com, or www.ibethel.org, or phone us at 530-246-6000.

More Exciting Titles
from Bill Johnson

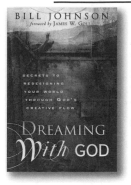

DREAMING WITH GOD

Dreaming with God is about releasing the people of God to their eternal purposes as co-laborers with Christ. He is interested in our desires, and would like for us to partner with Him in the unfolding of world events. The fullness of the Spirit obtained in intimacy is what qualifies us for such a role of influence.

ISBN 0-7684-2399-6

SUPERNATURAL POWER OF A TRANSFORMED MIND

Healing, deliverance, and signs and wonders are an inheritance for all followers of Jesus Christ. Johnson shows how to remove the blinders of religious limitation to redeem the lost and transform communities. You too can tap into that abundance of miricle-working authority and unleash the power of God's glory.

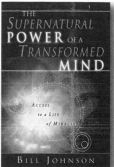

ISBN 0-7684-2252-3

WHEN HEAVEN INVADES EARTH

When Heaven Invades Earth is a powerful statement and testimony on the Kingdom of God. Theologically sound, well supported, and extremely well argued, this message provides a carefully constructed biblical foundation for the average Christian to live and walk in the miraculous power of God.

ISBN 0-7684-2952-8

SHIFTING SHADOWS OF SUPERNATURAL POWER

The voices of veteran prophets and healers release discernment and insights to the comming storm—a showdown with the modern prophets of Baal—in the church and in the world. Are you willing to step into the firestorm of total surrender, embrace the radiant presence of God, and prepare for an increase in authority and power?

ISBN 0-7684-2369-4

Available at your local Christian bookstore.

Additional copies of this book and other
book titles from DESTINY IMAGE are
available at your local bookstore.

Call toll free: 1-800-722-6774.

Send a request for a catalog to:

Destiny Image® Publishers, Inc.
P.O. Box 310
Shippensburg, PA 17257-0310

*"Speaking to the Purposes of God for this
Generation and for the Generations to Come."*

**For a complete list of our titles,
visit us at www.destinyimage.com**